T-SHIRT makeovers

20 Transformations for Fabulous Fashions

T·SHIRT makeovers
20 Transformations for Fabulous Fashions

SISTAHS OF HARLEM

CARMIA MARSHALL

AND CARMEN WEBBER

Glitterati
INCORPORATED

NEW YORK, NEW YORK

First published in the United States of America in 2006
by Glitterati Incorporated

225 Central Park West
New York, New York 10024
www.GlitteratiIncorporated.com

First edition, 2006

Library of Congress Control Number: 2006925132

Hardcover ISBN 0-9777531-7-4

Creative Direction by: David Yoon, Design by: Nancy Leonard
Photographs by: Derrick Gomez, www.derrickgomez.com

Printed and bound in China by Hong Kong Graphics & Printing Ltd.

10 9 8 7 6 5 4 3 2 1

······································

We dedicate this book to all aspiring fashion designers,

Remember:

1. Go for it

2. Never hold back

3. Never give up

4. Embrace who you are

5. Share it **Fearlessly** with the world

20 Transformations for Fabulous Fashions

CONTENTS

Chapter 1

T-shirt Philosophy

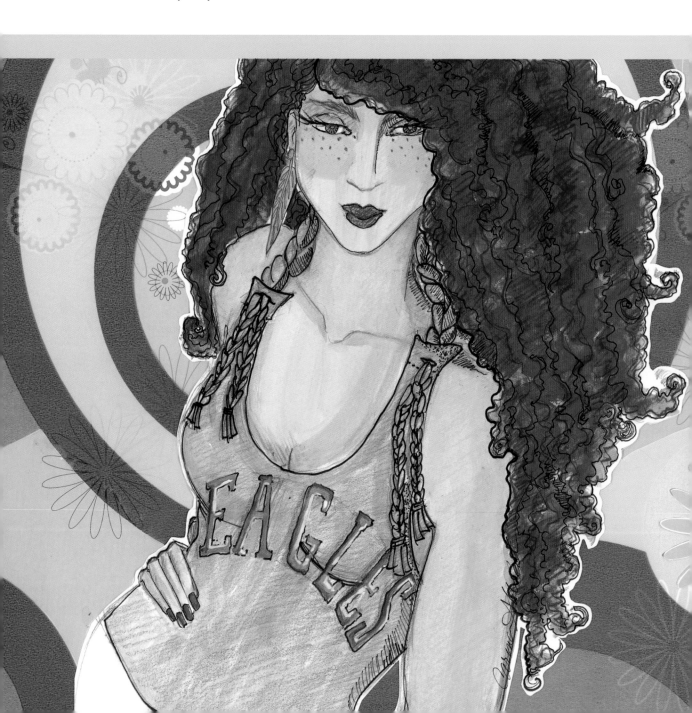

Old and worn, new or vintage, hip-hop, old school or modern classic, here's the 411 on today's most wearable item—the t-shirt. Everyone loves them, they are cute, comfortable, sophisticated, stylish, funky, and, not to mention incredibly versatile. The t-shirt in many ways is like the essential little black dress. You can dress it up or down, wear it to a club, the movies, athletic events, or even to the Oscars (remember how Sharon Stone rocked a white t-shirt at the award show and had the fashion tongues wagging for weeks). We are here to take your tees to an entire new plateau—reworked, embellished, and "funkdified."

For many young people, most of our wardrobe is t-shirts—they're everything! You always want to wear that t-shirt that you feel pretty in, that you feel sexy in, and that doesn't limit your movement. You can move comfortably in it because most t-shirts are cotton and cotton breathes. You don't feel stuck in a piece of plastic.

Why does everyone love t-shirts? They're comfortable, *extremely* comfortable. They can be irresistible; they can be snazzy. Like chameleons, they adapt to any environment. T-shirt flexibility is a definite plus. If you're like most people, you own dozens of t-shirts.

Recently, there's been a crossover between the t-shirt and the jersey. Jerseys are usually made of a material like a polyester blend or lycra blend, not just pure cotton. Speaking of blends, we love the new lycra/cotton. It's the best invention ever because you have stretch, yet the comfort of cotton. Lycra-cotton breathes, almost like pure cotton! The things the textile and apparel manufacturing industries are doing now with t-shirts are taking the humble tees to a whole 'nother level.

The evolution of t-shirt decoration is just as amazing. In the 60s, 70s and early 80s, tie-dye was all the craze. (It is a funky staple that will always come back in fashion, and there are many wonderful ways to rework a tie-dyed t-shirt.) Then folks took tie-dyeing a step further into silk screening and graphic design. The uses of rubber and reliefs on tees—

where the actual imagery or letters lift up from the fabric slightly when you rub your hand over it—are just fascinating. The technology of silk screening and printing t-shirts has brought sophistication and high creativity to once-humble tees.

We love doing fabulous things with t-shirts. We cut them and design them, dress them up and down, wear them as dresses or skirts and make super sporty jersey outfits. We've done t-shirts that are elaborate enough to wear to the Grammy Awards. Once beads could only be found on evening wear, but now beads are seen on t-shirts. We love to create a feminine look from something plain by adding sequins and all kinds of funky beads. And we're glad you can still embrace old t-shirts— ones your grandmamma had, ones your mother wore—and make them stylishly yours. To us, the evolution of the t-shirt has been a fashion opportunity.

Besides, we get so attached to our t-shirts. A lot of them cannot be replaced. They're old, aged, and distressed to perfection (you know that worn-in look that costs a fortune to manu- facture), not to mention one-of-a-kind! To trash our t-shirts would be like tossing out priceless treasures. However, we cannot deny that some shapes and forms become dated, although they do have sentimental value. This is where we come in and show you how to flip out your old t-shirts into stunning creations.

Favorite Tees

When I (Carmia) was in high school I used to play in our annual junior vs. senior powder puff game. I loved wearing red oversized football jerseys. They were very masculine and emphasized the feminine form as only a man's t-shirt hugging a woman's body in the right places can. I still have that jersey. I can convert that into something spectacular. Another t-shirt I cherish is one I wore when I was a dancer at Creative Expression Dance Studio. It is just a plain baggy t-shirt, displaying the Creative Expression logo, that we wore at dance competitions, but it means so much to me because I competed and traveled all over in that t-shirt. Now I can make that ten-year-old t-shirt fashionable and cute just by changing its shape.

I (Carmen) love quirky t-shirts—my family reunion t-shirt, the one designed for that company baseball team or a corporate summer picnic or sales event, the contest t-shirts with kooky code names. We all love the real thing—sports team, celebrity, and favorite brand name shirts—but kitsch and comical ones are fun, too. My favorites are ones for religious summer school and little day camp tees. They are just too adorable.

Speaking of celebrity oriented t-shirts, ones from concerts become very valuable over the years. If you have an original t-shirt from a David Bowie, Mick Jagger, or Prince's Purple Rain concert, it is valuable, and you want to be careful to really freak it! It's great to see the influence that music

and politics have had on t-shirts. Over the years tees have been more than functional. Tees have become a form of expression, a *voice*. They've become an activist voice, playing a visible role in accomplishing change in our world.

T-shirt Style Makes the Old New and Lets the Tee "Speak"

Sometimes you have old tees that you consider giving to charity or just throwing away, but you can't part with them. You can't see yourself wearing it because it's unstylish or on its last strings, but you can't get rid of it, either. We have a solution. Our motto is "bring us anything and we can save it."

We fell in love with old t-shirts and we change their shape and make them something completely different, yet preserve what we love about them. With very little sewing, you can make that beloved t-shirt your own thing—reinvent it, change its shape, let it find its true personality.

One of our customers, Dhevi, had this really old gray t-shirt she didn't want to throw away. It was one of her college t-shirts. It was frayed and even ripped under the armpits. We added appliqués, took material from the sleeves and totally patch-worked it, using beautiful hard stitching. We gave it a quilted effect around the arm and bodice. That old favorite tee became a new wardrobe staple for her.

Even when we're shopping for new shirts we pick up on a tee's vibration before we deconstruct a t-shirt. It sounds weird, but each shirt has its own personality. If the shirt ends up looking like a walking arts-and-crafts project, hand-painted and very colorful, it's because that most expresses the t-shirt's original character. Your creativity is supposed to bring out the tee's best. That's what we as designers call t-shirt style. It's way beyond wearable art. T-shirt style lets you merge your clothing style with your favorite wearables.

Deconstructing/Reconstructing

When deconstructing a t-shirt you're just not limited to revamping, making the t-shirt a different shape. You can make it into an accessory—a hand bag, scarf, belt, arm warmer, wrist bands, headband, hair wraps. It only needs to be suited to your body, your wardrobe, your personal statement. The amount of care you take to choose a style and make an artisan's approach to a tee is worth it because you're preserving something sentimental or just making something that feels great and expresses *you*. But it doesn't take much time. You'll see from our instructions that most of the deconstructing and reconstructing can be done in one sitting. Some don't even require a sewing machine—but having one really helps!

Always save your scraps!

Top-Shelf Tees

No one would have imagined years ago that there would be such a huge crossover from ready-to-wear to couture fashion. Huge fashion houses in Paris, Milan, and London are totally copying hip-hop street life. T-shirts play a large role in that. It's incredible that couture is so hip-hop and urban based! People are definitely *not* wearing t-shirts just to slop around in, go to the grocery store, or work in the garden. Tees are dressed!

There was a time when you would never pay more than ten or fifteen dollars for a t-shirt. Now they go up to $200. (The ones you make from our instructions will look like those multi-Benjamin buys, but you can make them for a few dollars.)

The mileage you get out of a t-shirt is unbelievable. T-shirts from the 40s and 50s are still around because they're durable—the cotton on those oldies is soft and luxurious. Today's tees should hold up just as long.

T-shirts are no longer inappropriate to wear in the workplace, and the way we deconstruct some tees, they're totally at home in the workplace—with or without a blazer. And then, when you leave work, you've got on this hot cute top to transition you to your next destination.

Wearing t-shirts now says, "I'm comfortably chic." The evolution of the t-shirt has been a fashion diva's godsend. We love to create a myriad of looks from something as plain as a basic white tee. Even more,

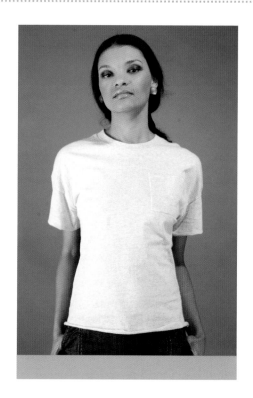

we're glad you can still embrace old t-shirts—ones your grandmamma had, ones your mother wore, even your dad's old gym tees—and make them stylishly yours. To us the evolution of the t-shirt has been a fashion opportunity.

Of course, we still love the basic tee. We love to pair a plain t-shirt with jeans, or slacks or cute skirt; but we also love to jazz it up and make it look fabulous. People stop us on the street and ask, "Where did you get that t-shirt? Who did it?" This book is so you gals (or boys making tops for gals) can have the option of wearing fabulous tees in your personal t-shirt style.

A GREAT SENSE OF FASHION STARTS WITH A STATE OF..... MIND

GIAS STATE OF MIND 5

SIMPLE WHITE TEE

● ● ●

A great sense of fashion starts with a state of mind.

my t-shir[...]
hot poetry.
   They move[...]
provoking tha[...]
non-apologe[...]
   for they stan[...]
something, enc[...]
touch many.
   They make[...]
think. They[...]
entertain a[...]
   educate. [...]
Most have[...]
   message[...]
that I h[...]
   heart.
Persona[...]
simple[...]
yet f[...]
my t-shirts are like poetry.

ZORA 5

A T-SHIRT POEM:

* * *

My t-shirts are not poetry.
They move freely,
provoking thought—
non-apologetic—
for they stand for something,
encourage, touch many.
They make you laugh, cry, think.
They entertain and educate.
Most have a message
that I hold close to my heart.
Personal, priceless, simple,
yet full of twists and turns,
my t-shirts are like poetry.

Chapter 2
Love Your Body

All designers—from the House of Gucci to Yves St. Laurent to the street couture designers of Sistahs of Harlem—have one crucial thing in common: we express our ideas for a collection by using various silhouettes, the outline of natural contours of the body. The frames you see dancing manically to the rhythm in iPOD commercials are silhouettes. Your silhouette is your body profile. For Sistahs of Harlem, our silhouettes are found in the eclectic streets of New York City. The styles we create have everything to do with how it works on the body. When designing your fabulous t-shirts, it is important to think of your silhouette, the contour of your body, and what will flatter you the most.

First and foremost, realize that you are beautiful from head to toe; every inch of you is designed perfection, so adore yourself and your body wholeheartedly. Our bodies are as diverse as the beautiful world we live in. There are no "right" or "wrong" body types. Each type deserves unabashed celebration. Wear your clothes with confidence, and wear clothes that flatter you.

You want to know what distinguishes good fit for any body at any size? Clothing that skims the outline of your beautiful shape, nothing that clings, tugs, or pulls the body, nor anything over-sized that hides the curves of your body's natural lines. Know who you are and how to work your t-shirt design to the flyest. Create with your body type in mind.

Bombshell Extraordinaire

Otherwise known as the hourglass. Curvy. Balanced hip and shoulder width with a defined waist. Marilyn Monroe, Halle Berry, Selma Hayek, Beyonce, Kirstie Alley are lovely examples of Bombshell Extraordinaires, ranging from petite to full-figured (Marilyn Monroe was a size 12! You go, big girl!)

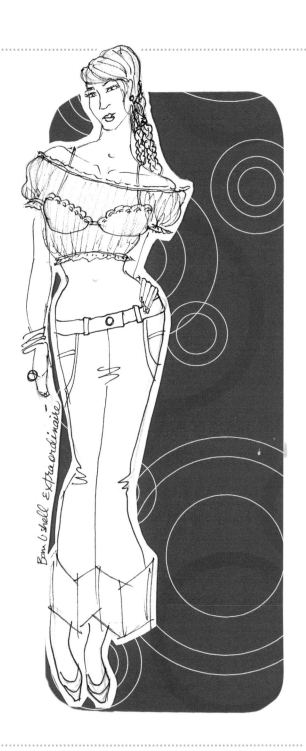

You can rock any style t-shirt. Every neckline will look good on you. So try them all, crew neck, scoop neck, a boat neck, to name a few. Your biggest concern is to stay away from ill-fitted shirts, but do not confuse too tight with nice formfitting silhouettes. Remember to pump up the positive!

Gracefully Voluptuous

A.k.a. full-figured. Jill Scott, Raven Simone, Starr Jones, Kelly Osbourne, Tocarra from "America's Next Top Model," Mia Tyler, Camryn Manheim, and Queen Latifah.

You want to wear shirts that minimize the abdomen area. This does not mean forsaking fashion with oversized t-shirts that lack shape and form.

Rock baby doll shirts, dramatic raglan or kimono sleeves work well and bishop and peasant sleeves with slim-fitted silhouettes are positively complementary, and blouson style shirts are an absolute must. Avoid clingy styles that interrupt your natural silhouette.

Sporty Spitfire

An inverted triangle, you have average to broad shoulders wider than your hips, and a straight, short-to-average waist. Kelly Rowland, Keira Knightly, Mischa Barton, Eve, Madonna, Cameron Diaz, Angela Bassett, Venus and Serena Williams are Sporty Spitfires.

T-shirts made over for a tailored look are great on you. They help to create your waist. Don't be afraid to add a sash to your t-shirt or tailor it to fit to perfection. You can wear all necklines from crews, scoops, to boat necks.

Miss Balance

You are a rectangle, hip and shoulders balanced, with no defined waist. Angelina Jolie, Penelope Cruz, Jennifer Connelly, Michelle Williams from Destiny's Child and Jada Pinkett-Smith are examples.

Your biggest concern is your minimal waistline. Don't fret. There are many ways to exaggerate your waist. To create a waistline, you want to work with tailored t-shirts. They are hot on you and define your waist with little effort. Utilize corset-like accessories—which can be made from t-shirt materials such as *obi* style belts. *Obi* style belts are similar to the traditional Japanese kimono waist belt. Often wide and pulled tight around the waist, this belt is an excellent example of a slightly synched waist to give the illusion of a defined waist. They can be made out of t-shirt scraps. Stay tuned and we'll teach you how to do this. One thing is for sure: you should go crazy with the necklines. You can rock the basics: crew neck, V-neck, and scoop neck.

Perfectly Pear

You are a triangle, shoulders narrower than hips, slim torso and ribcage, small waist, full lower hips. Alicia Keys, Debra Messing, and Kerry Washington are examples of lovely pears. Your biggest concern is your full hips. (Some of us wouldn't consider this a problem. Hello!) Camouflaging the hips isn't hard, if that's what you want to do. Wear shirts that hit at the upper hip. By doing this you eliminate chopping yourself in half. If a shirt bares midriff, you bring attention to the belly and hips. If this is not what you're looking for, avoid shirts too short. You can also model A-line shirts. These types of lovely shirts drape over your hips nicely. They're always charming and lively. Baby doll shirts also rock the body well.

Let's move up the body chart and address your shoulders. Your shoulders are a little narrow so if you want to add more girth put shoulder details on your tee. Play with puff sleeves, epaulets, and ruffles to name a few.

● ● ●

T-shirt makeovers can enhance your natural silhouette. We want to complement, not complicate, your t-shirt wardrobe—well, maybe we'll make it a *little bit* complex. We want to help you step it up.

Perfectly Pear

ACCESSORIES

This book shows you how to create t-shirts that are specifically for you, so here are some secrets on how to use tees to flatter your upper body and enhance your natural silhouette. It's all about flattery. We will show you how to play up your body assets to the highest level. If you follow these tricks, you will be a happy fashionista in a couture t-shirt made exclusively for you and your body.

Face trick:

A round face and a round neckline equal a rounder face. A square face and a square neckline equal a more square face. To accentuate the shape of your face, wear the same neckline. To minimize the shape of your face, wear a contrasting neckline. If the shape of your face is drastic in any way, refrain from repeating this shape in your neckline. Wear a contrasting neckline to create balance, a more attractive line. It's your face! It's one of the first things we see. Hypnotize all those you desire with striking good looks and the right t-shirt.

Neck tips:

If your neck is long, and you love it, you can wear the entire gamut of necklines from scoop, v, turtle, mock, tie, cowl and mandarin collars. So go crazy and enjoy the versatility of wearing whatever neckline you're in the mood for. If you desire to shorten your long gorgeous neck, try choker necklines and other styles worn close to the neck.

If you need to lengthen a short neck, wear V-necks or open collars and flaunt longer necklaces to expose more of the neckline area. This will elongate the neck. When dressed correctly, you look taller. You stand stronger and more poised. Your head is up and your neck is exposed and boy does it look tantalizing! Work the neck. It's the best-kept secret on the body!

Arm tricks:

Everyone can wear a long sleeve. It's the easiest sleeve to pull off. Here's the skinny on the short-sleeve tee, it should be either one inch above or below the bust line. To disguise short arms you need to wear three-quarter sleeves. It seems like an awkward sleeve length, but this sleeve really looks good on shorter arms. It lengthens your arms in a subtle manner. Not everyone should fall totally in love with the three-quarter tee. Be careful if you have long arms; this sleeve elongates your arms and is not always flattering on us beauties with long limbs. They can cut your arms in half in an unflattering manner. Nothing else is off limits—wear it all from the most dramatic of dramatic sleeves— you have the limbs to pull it off! To slenderize thick arms, wear tapered, set-in long sleeves or raglan sleeves. A set-in sleeve is cut separately from the waist of the garment and sewed directly to the armhole. In other words, it's a simple straight sleeve. A raglan sleeve extends the neckline and has a slanting seam line from the underarm to neck in front and back. These sleeves hide the unwanted jiggle on our arms. To camouflage long thin arms, wear layers. A fitted layer will add girth in a fashionably strong manner. Wear long or raglan style sleeves, blousy or peasant sleeves. Two thumbs up to these free flowing sleeves—including those on our long sleeve Missy shirt in Chapter 18.

Bust tips: Some of us have them. Some of us don't. Let's take what we have and make the best of it. For all the ladies with cup sizes A and B, here are some clues to enhance your bust: wear fitting bodice shirts, use breasts enhancers to slip into your bra, and padded bras are great for a clean smooth look. Enjoy the versatility of being able to wear more sleek and sultry shirts that may require losing the bra. One thing to avoid for sure is low cut shirts that reveal too much cleavage. For the women who have been blessed with full bust and seek to minimize, avoid horizontal lines at bust level; rock blouson styles that skim your natural bust line; interesting necklines to pull attention away from your breast, and also t-shirts that taper softly under the breast. Vertical lines minimize a large bust, as do open collars and V-necks. Here is a great fashion tip: invest in a fitted support bra or minimizer, because a good bra can work wonders for your breasts by lifting them up and creating outstanding shape. Excellent support equals more shirt options.

Your breasts are your breasts. Celebrate them in a way that keeps others guessing what's really behind the shirt.

Shoulder tricks: To broaden shoulders, add any type of shoulder detail to increase the width of your shoulders. Puff sleeves, epaulets, raglan, leg-o-mutton, and peasant sleeves will all add volume to your shoulders. Wear very wide or shallow necklines. A shallow neck, meaning not deep, draws the eyes out. To those who have broad shoulders, we want you to flaunt the hell out of them! Broad shoulders are rock star! They provide you with extreme versatility. However, if you choose to minimize, avoid wide or shallow necklines. Wear deep scoop necks or low V-necks. This trick will bring more focus to the neckline instead of the shoulders.

Waist tips: To minimize a thick waist and diminish a prominent tummy—and still have fun!— look for straight, body skimming styles that obscure the waist. Roll out your baby doll styles, blouson styles. They are flattering styles that work well for your body. Avoid anything that sticks to the abdomen area. Clingy shirts are not a good look.

Understanding your body shape and creating your "ultimate" silhouette takes time. It's an ongoing process. As we evolve and grow, our styles change and so do our bodies. One thing remains true, once you understand how to control the natural contours of your body, you will look and feel matchless in your t-shirt.

ACCESSORIES

● ● ●

From the most chic women to the edgiest sistahs everyone adores a great scarf.

Chapter 3
Kaleidoscopic Closet

Colors are infinite. Colors are true. We will not tell a lie. We crave colors. Our closets are an enchanting kaleidoscope. Hues of every kind are woven into a striking palette. Bold and brilliant colors greet you from every corner. The rainbow landed in our closet space and decided not to leave. Sistahs of Harlem love, love, love vivacious colors—electric blue, cherry red, canary yellow, kelly green. Color is a magic ingredient that makes your t-shirt wardrobe work.

A stash of t-shirts is a simple way to make sure you are always wearing the colors that are best for you. To have a t-shirt in every color is not excessive. It is fashion savvy. (You don't have to buy brand new t-shirts. You can replenish your tees from the local Salvation Army.) Different circumstances call for different color tees. Your tees can take you from the weekly morning meeting at your workplace to the social scene where you let go.

Why are Sistahs of Harlem sooooooooooo color happy?

Colors alone are a form of expression. Since we *want* to express ourselves, we cannot help falling in love with the color wheel. When creating new seasonal collections, we discuss our color schemes in mad detail. It is *crucial* in the development of our line. Colors create atmosphere. Colors determine a mood. They tell stories of power, love, tranquility, nature, and sensuality. Before we even cut a t-shirt we observe its color. Tees allow us to simply and inexpensively vary the statements we make with our clothes. We can't ignore it. Colors move. Colors stand. Colors speak.

Diane, a new friend of ours, always wore black. Every time we saw her she wore some rendition of a black uniform and it wasn't job related. She was a gorgeous girl with a dismal wardrobe. She was a definite mover and shaker, pursuing her dreams as an architect, always admirable, but her wardrobe did not reflect her charismatic personality. One day, we bumped into Diane at Settepani, a great coffee shop in Harlem. We decided to share tea. Of course, we could not resist asking, "Why do you always wear black?" It was mid-July and 80 degrees outside. We shortly discovered Diane was depressed about her break-up with her fiancé of two years. She had gained a few pounds and decided to wear black since it was a slimming color. We totally understood her pain, but ladies and gents, this is no excuse to wear black every day. There are other ways to disguise your body's

shortcomings. Wearing black *every day* isn't the only way. Love your body and it's changes, always and forever! We consoled her as we continued to exchange quick life updates. We promised to keep in touch. We kept it moving because we had a meeting with a buyer and we couldn't be late.

A month later, Diane called us and said she was ready for a makeover. She wanted a new direction, more inspiration, and had decided to start with her wardrobe. We were thrilled. We were beyond ready to hook this diva up with some fresh gear. We went directly to her closet. To our surprise, she owned tons of colored t-shirts. We reworked her tees into a variety of styles and black become obsolete in her closet. The rest is history! Diane rocks color daily.

Now don't get us wrong. Black is a swank color. It definitely has a place in your t-shirt wardrobe. However, we encourage you to explore the rainbow. Avoid limiting yourself to one hue. You do not have to be as extreme as Diane was or color junkies like us, but the truth remains that utilizing color in your T-robe is an asset. (See color chart opposite page)

T-shirts come in a variety of blends. Some are pure cotton; others are lycra/cotton, polyester/cotton and linen/cotton and silk/cotton. The combos are endless. Based on fabric content, certain tees hold color in different ways. Pure cotton fades. It's all natural so it has the tendency to lose color faster than the other t-shirt blends. Pay attention to care labels. But, if you have a favorite colored tee, we recommend you hand wash it. Don't risk losing the color.

LET'S REVIEW THE COLOR BASICS

● ● ●

Primary colors: red, yellow, and blue

Secondary colors: orange, green and purple

Neutrals: beige and stone (These colors are almost invisible.)

Achromatic colors: black and white

Sometimes the care label instructions are "machine wash cold, tumble dry" and I (Carmia) completely ignore it. I want to know that my shirt is okay. I can't see inside the machine as it washes. I know this must sound neurotic, but I obviously had a bad experience. It was 1998, I went to my Summer bi-annual family reunion. My cousin Brian had designed our tees and I was proud. The t-shirt was hot pink and the silk screening was tight! Can you imagine a herd of hot pink tees in the park in Tennessee? I misplaced this t-shirt and found it five years later. Of course, I had to re-work it to be F&F (fierce and fab). I loved the reworked halter t-shirt so much. I washed the shirt in cold water with mild detergent and the shirt faded like Casper, the friendly ghost. My cousin may have dyed the shirt incorrectly, but this doesn't matter. If I had suspected that this would happen, I would have hand washed the tee without question. Yes, the color would have faded but not as much. I could have worn it at least ten more times! Traumatic,

but I learned the hard way that special shirts require special care.

Again, check the care label. Things like this don't always occur. Losing some color is unavoidable. You can't fight natural wear and tear. Needless to say, favorite tees should be hand washed and hung dry, especially if you want to maintain the color. Another great tip, if you have fancy embellishments or silk screening on your tee, turn it inside out and wash them. This helps to preserve the artwork while eliminating the dirt.

Some t-shirts are so extravagant that they require dry cleaning. Dry-clean t-shirts?! Yep, that's right. The silk screening can be a masterpiece and such bling embellishments need ultimate attention. As a result, professionals become mandatory. You also can recommend to your dry cleaner to turn your t-shirts inside out in order to preserve the art. The maintenance of your tee is crucial. Do what you have to do but keep your t-shirt colors looking right.

Colors as Moods

Colors are diverse as the personalities of the individuals who wear them. They evoke the scope of emotions since we relate certain colors to various events in our lives. When I (Carmen) want to chill or lay low, I wear colors in the blue family. Blues are so calming to me. I'll never forget my first trip to Wilmington Beach in North Carolina. My mother and I were sailing in the sea. Soothing blue water surrounded me.

Little rainbows were scattered across the ocean since the sun reflected on the water. The skies were crystal blue. The air was light, breezy, and clean. The endless canvas of blue was mesmerizing. It was the most relaxing moment of my childhood. Every time I want to relive this moment, I wear blue, my color of serenity.

SISTAHS OF HARLEM T-SHIRT COLOR AURORA GUIDE

● ● ●

Red evokes passion, energy, fire, electricity, and power.

Blue is cooling, calming, sober, spiritual, and lucid.

Yellow is vibrant, sassy, and simultaneous and playful.

Purple is regal, courageous, magical, noble, and undeniable.

Green reflects healing, prosperity, rebirth, and generosity.

Orange is optimism, confidence, tolerancce, brilliance, and pleasure.

White is pure, serenity, meditative, innocent, and dreamy.

Black is no-nonsense, professional, sophisticated and silent; receptive, classy, and timeless.

Your tees can be your color aurora. The types of colors that you wear can communicate your feelings without speaking a word. Believe it or not, those around will notice and pick up on your energy based upon the colors you wear in the moment.

You want colors to help express a certain feeling. Your juiced up tee can do this for you.

Color is contagious. It spreads like wild fire and will brighten your entire existence. Embrace the rainbow. Your closet will feel the difference.

Color Identity

You wear the right colors. Your skin is flawless. Your eyes glow gracefully and your hair appears to be having the perfect hair day no matter how it's behaving. You experience a sense of freedom and freshness. Excellent color makes you powerful.

You wear the wrong color and your complexion deadens. Unnatural shadows cloud your face as well as magnify under-eye circles. Your skin looks pale and your inner diva is drowned by painful unwanted color. You look flat and one-dimensional. Bad color makes you disappear into the background. Poof! You're gone.

We want you to understand what color does for your wardrobe and your body because tees in the right colors hit the bull's-eye.

Color Theory 101

Check it out. Colors paint our world. We cannot control it. Grass is green. Water is blue. Fire is red. Night is black. We can't alter the colors of nature no matter how hard we try. Colors, vast in hue, shade, and intensity make up the universe. According to Johannas Itten, "Color is life, for a world without color seems dead. As a flame produces light, light produces color. . . ." We

categorize colors into groups in hopes of identifying with them. We can't help associating certain colors with various occurrences in life. Certain hues signify certain elements of living. It's undeniable.

We use these terms regularly. Jog your memory bank. How many times have you called your home girl and confessed your need for a bright colored t-shirt? You needed a loud color that's in-your-face and noticeable. We constantly describe the types of colors we want to wear without knowing it.

LET'S BREAK THIS DOWN.

● ● ●

Hot Think lava red. It is the essence of fire.

Cool Visualize ice and water with combined colors of blue and green.

Dark See the black night and shadows. It's strong and melancholy.

Warm Experience a sunset, with yellow tones.

Light Touch sand. It's barely visible.

Pale Enjoy pink cotton candy, soft, feminine and pastel, mixed with white.

Bright Eye-popping neon colors. Clear, high chrome and vivid. You can't ignore them.

Your Color

We all have color palettes and are naturally drawn to certain colors. It's an innate character of being human. Your color palette can be broken into four-color season categories: winter, spring, summer, or fall. Before we explore the four-color season palettes, let's determine your skin tone. Your skin tone is the coloring underneath your skin. Your skin tone is synonymous to your complexion. It is the tone just under the surface that determines your "skin tone."

The tone of your skin comes from three pigments: melanin (brown), carotene (yellow), and hemoglobin (red). The combination of these pigments determines your innate skin tone.

The Skin Tone Test

Look at yourself in natural light. No make-up. No clothes. Pull your hair up and away from your face. Hold up a piece of silver and gold metallic swatches (a sample piece of fabric) to your face. If you have a large piece, wrap it around your neck and shoulders. Do so one at a time. If gold is more flattering, your skin tone is warm (which is tagged "red"). If silver is more complimentary, your skin tone is cool (which is tagged "blue").

How do you know what looks good on you? First, it's intuitive. You will look at yourself and recognize, hands down, this is one of the colors for me. Thank the genius Johannes Itten for his revolutionary approach to color theory. Itten discovered that color harmony is quite individual, and that an individual will, if given free reign and a little knowledge, find his or her own "subjective colors." His discovery continues to influence the design world today. There's a little history for you. So you will recognize your skin tone; it's in your blood.

Second, you can see physical changes in your appearance immediately. Whether your skin tone is warm (red) or cool (blue), wear colors that match your complexion. You look radiant. A luminous glow is apparent. You and the colors are one.

When you sport colors opposite your skin tone, you look washed out and hardened. We want to avoid this as much as we can.

When you recognize your natural under tones, your ability to chose flattering colors triples. These are the moves we want to make.

Determine the Right Colors:

We all have a season that's complimentary to our skin tones. What season best reflects you?

Winter: Skin tone pink or blue. Rock, cool blue-based colors. Embrace clear colors. Clear, bright high chromatic color; pure hues are a dream. Flaunt: pure white, black, navy blue, emerald green, royal purple, magenta, not pink and bright burgundy. If it is a truly intense and bright color, you can work it. **Avoid** light and neutral and translucent colors. They blend into your skin in the worst way. Dismiss yellow-beiges, pastels such as pink and light yellow (yuck! for you), bronze, rust, peach, yellow beiges, and browns. **You look your best in** true, intense, bright vivid colors. Pale neutrals are less flattering.

Summer: Blue undertone w/ visible pink in your skin. You look for more softness than intense pure colors. This is the contrary to your winter counter part. Your best colors are blue based. In fact, you can wear every shade of blue except royal blue (too intense) for your complexion. Enjoy: soft white (no yellow undertones), the entire gamut of pinks, rose beiges, medium grays, the entire plum family, and light yellow. **Avoid:** pure colors such as black, pure white, and all colors with yellow

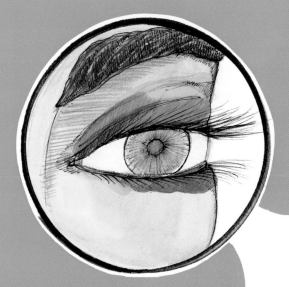

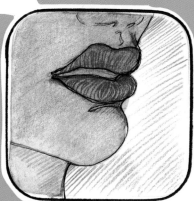

SKIN AND COLOR

• • •

A great sense of fashion starts with a state of mind.

undertones. **You look best in** soft neutrals; extremely feminine colors do wonders for you.

Autumn: golden undertones in skin. Your middle name is yellow-based. You can run the spectrum of yellow-based colors. Lucky girl, you can wear anything with a golden undertone. **Your color palette** has the widest range of colors. Golden tones make you look brilliant. Let them know you're coming with the entire family of browns (in fact, chocolate should be your new black), mahogany, camel, pumpkin, mustard, chartreuse, oyster, yellow, medium peach, orange, dark salmon, dark turquoise, deep periwinkle. All bronze tones are excellent for you. Earth greens, foreest greens, green in general truly shine on you skin. **Avoid** blue-based colors, such as black, navy, gray, blue-reds, and pink.

Spring: Golden undertone in skin; Bathe in warm yellow-based colors as your Autumn sister. The difference, however, is you require the lighter shade, than the autumn season. You can pull off the lightest of the lightest colors with yellow bases. Your nickname is the queen of light. You require crystal clear colors, such as clear turquoise, light true blue, peach, salmon, coral, golden tan, and milk chocolate. Dress in light orange, light gray with yellow undertones, ivory, peacock blue (it's about the only blue that you can wear), and all peachy pinks. **Avoid** black, pure white, and colors with blue undertones. Your colors are harder to find, but you're blessed with delicate crystal clear skin that lasts the test of time.

When you find a tee in "your" color, buy it in multiples and make it over into dozens of flattering styles and use that colored tee as a base to wear other clothes that you adore—but are not the right color for you.

Your skin tone is the blue print for determining what colors look F&F and gorgeous on you. Your tees should highlight your skin tone to make you look most luminous.

Monochromatic Tees

Monochromatic tees a.k.a. solid colored t-shirts have a legit place in your armoire. Some days you may not want to wear a patterned tee or any type of silk screening. You want a great style tee on a single colored shirt. Not a bad idea.

We preach jazz, jazz, jazz. We can't help it. It's what we do. But we also understand that there is a time and place for everything. Some days you want drama. Some days you don't. Not to mention, solid tees can be extremely slimming and camouflage your less attractive attributes. They compliment a variety of silhouettes, are safe and less likely to create a color faux pas. A great style in a solid color is an all around winner.

Colored Tees as Accents

Colored tees as accents are dazzling. They can add "oomph" and subtly or boldly evoke a myriad of emotions. They can draw attention in the right way and with little effort. A colored tee as an unexpected accessory is absolutely smashing. For instance, you're wearing all black. By adding a yellow tee or a simple black tee made over with royal blue flower appliqué, animal print or red trim, you create another dimension to your ensemble. It gives your black ensemble some panache and spunk. This is what we want.

Let's get to the nitty gritty and make over our t-shirts in a five-star manner.

Chapter 4
Quick Tee Makeover Tips

Quick Tee Makeover Tips A must-read for beginners and important reminders for the experienced t-shirt "maker-overer."

Tip #1: **Perfect ironing = great sewing.** Every single t-shirt to be revamped should be ironed properly.

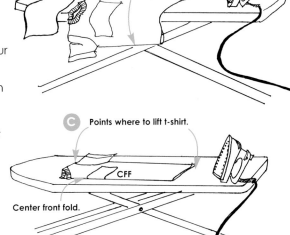

Side folds/seams.

Points where to lift t-shirt.

Center front fold.

CFF

A. If your t-shirt has any sort of printed or heat press image, you must use a pressing cloth! Place the cloth over the image when running the iron across your t-shirt. You can buy a pressing cloth or make your own with clean white cotton pillowcases or sheet fragments.

B. First, iron all wrinkles out. Make sure that sides are straight and not twisted. Most t-shirts do not have actual seam, so when you press them you will create side folds/seams. Throughout this book, those side folds are actually what we refer to as "side seams."

C. Once you have ironed your t-shirt perfectly flat, fold it with care. Here's the way to do this: Match up the sleeve insets (armpits), and fold your t-shirt directly in half. Place it flat on the ironing board or another large, smooth surface. This creates the center front fold, which we refer to as C.F.F. The center front fold is one of the formulas from which pattern drafting originates.

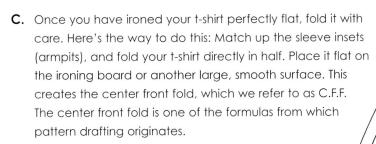

D. Most important, the wrong iron temperature can destroy an innocent shirt. Always regard labels for fabric content. With this info, you can be sure to set your iron on the right temperature, eliminating the chances of damaging your tees. Knowledge is power, peeps!

Tip#2 **Know the difference** between the correct versus the incorrect side of the fabric.

A. This is important for your clean or invisible seams. For example, the cross-hatching print = correct side of fabric. Stripes = reverse or back side of fabric.

B. For example, you will stitch on the reverse or back side of fabric unless directed otherwise.

C. When you turn the fabric inside out, you will get a clean or invisible seam. Invisible seams are actually visible when you look at the fabric closely. From a distance, they appear to be just clean lines.

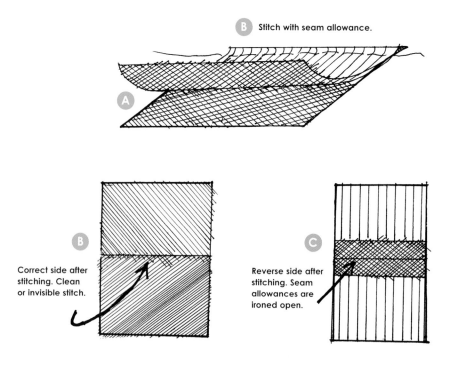

B Stitch with seam allowance.

Correct side after stitching. Clean or invisible stitch.

Reverse side after stitching. Seam allowances are ironed open.

Tip#3 **Get pins**. Proper use of straight pins is key when securing fabric in place before sewing.

A. Remember there are different straight pins for different fabrics and some fabrics are so delicate that you cannot use pins on them. So when you purchase your straight pins be sure to ask for a point size appropriate for cottons and satin. Often polyester and rayon have that same thin flowing weight, like satin or even silk. Some pins are longer than others, some even have little decorative pearls at the end.

B. Below is the direction you place your pins for different purposes.

cutting = vertical direction

sewing by hand = vertical direction

sewing by machine = horizontal direction

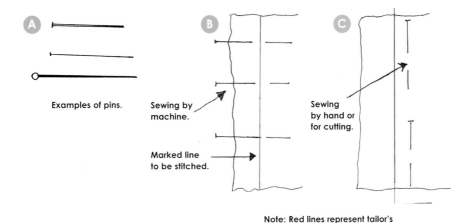

Examples of pins.

Sewing by machine.

Marked line to be stitched.

Sewing by hand or for cutting.

Note: Red lines represent tailor's chalk markings for sewing path.

Tip #4: **Cutting rules.** Once you cut, there's no turning back! Cutting mistakes are costly and irreversible.

A. Always give seam allowance. We suggest ¼" to ½" For example, when you measure and make your lines, be sure to include seam allowance. Or you have the option to not include it in your measurements and add the ¼" or ½" allowance as you cut.

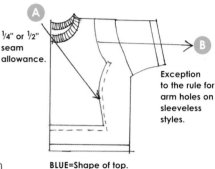

¼" or ½" seam allowance.

Exception to the rule for arm holes on sleeveless styles.

BLUE=Shape of top.

RED=Cutting path with seam allowance

B. The exception to the seam allowance rule is for sleeveless t-shirts; you can cut directly on the arm hole line. But remember you must still give seam allowance for side seams always.

C. Always cut on flat clean surfaces. The bottom blade of your scissor should always be against a flat plane. Never cut on your lap or in the air.

D. Fabric scissors versus paper scissors—believe it or not, blades do get dull over time. Establish which scissor is for fabric use and which is for paper use. NEVER EVER use your fabric scissor on paper! The blades must stay sharp so that you will get a perfect, precise fabric cutting. Never use paper scissors on fabric. It will not be sharp enough.

E. A seam ripper will become your new best friend. This device allows you to remove stitches from a seam effortlessly. They are easy to find and worth the investment. ($3.00 at your local drugstore.) They also help to eliminate tearing or ripping your stitch when trying to remove a seam. Carefully, use the pointed end to pick the stitches out. Once you have eliminated a stitch with the point, gently push the seam ripper forward, the stitches come flying out. Keep your seam ripper by your side.

Bottom of blade flat against table/surface.

CENTER FRONT FOLD

Tip #5 Measurements

A. Your proper measurements are crucial for the perfect fit. Here as follows is the list of needed measurements for your t-shirt makeover:

1. neck to waist front
2. neck to waist back
3. bust
4. waist
5. upper hip
6. hip
7. shoulder to center armpit

Remember everyone's torso will vary as some of us are short waisted.

Shoulder to center armpit.

Bust.

Waist.

6"

9"

B. Since everything is cut on the fold, bust, waist, and both hip measurements should be divided by 4 to get the proper distance from center front and back folds. The shoulder to the center armpit is the only measurement that will remain the same.

For example:

Measurement equation answer

Bust	34" ÷ 4 =	$8\frac{1}{2}$"
Waist	27" ÷ 4 =	$6\frac{3}{4}$"
Upper hip	35" ÷ 4 =	$8\frac{3}{4}$"
Hip	37" ÷ 4 =	$9\frac{1}{4}$"

C. Your upper hip measurement is normally 6" from your belly button. Your true hip measurement is normally 9" from your belly button.

D. Super Cheat—you can simply take a tank top or shirt that fits you perfectly, fold it in half, and take those measurements to get the fit you like. Just take into consideration that the measurements taken by hand will be more accurate.

Tip #6: Trial & Error

As with anything, practice makes perfect. We suggest a trial run on some of the more difficult styles. Use a throw-away tee (something you're not attached to) or a completely tattered t-shirt before actually cutting into your favorite t-shirt.

  Or practice different techniques on one XL or even 2XL t-shirt to get the hang of things. On that same t-shirt, practice cutting perfect lines.

Tip #7 Get the Science

We have a good glossary. Take advantage of it. Be sure that you understand the techniques before proceeding with a project.

Tip #8 Essentials

Findings and tools are needed. We have made a list of findings and tools needed for each style. As with cooking, make sure you have all your ingredients before you begin the project!

Tip #9 Save the Scraps

Keep all the scraps and cut-away fabric from your made-over tees. It'll come in handy as you improvise on our designs and become a tee-designing diva yourself.

Tip #10 Quick Cheats

Please realize that a lot of the techniques used in this book are short cuts from traditional sewing methods. The idea is to make this a cool experience with a quick fix to funky fun fashion. That said, don't get too excited and skip important information and steps. We sometimes have a tendency to look at the pretty pictures and sketches without reading.

Enjoy and happy sewing!

Chapter 5

Elizabeth

Simple Scoop Top

The Elizabeth top is a great "girl-next-door" t-shirt. The deep scoop neck tee, with short slashed sleeves and small ribbons that tie at the shoulder, is simply charming. You can even use the shoulder ties to secure your tee to your bra to prevent it from falling off the shoulder.

Some days I (Carmia) like to keep it simple without compromising my fashion integrity. The Elizabeth top allows me to have the comfort of a plain tee with a little pizzazz. I'll never forgot the time I ran out of my apartment last summer to drop off my dry cleaning before closing. In a hurry, I grabbed my purse, and the to-be laundered garments. Little did I know that I left my keys on the kitchen table and the automatic lock on the door. Bad! My homie, who has keys to the apartment, was at a birthday party in the city, and would not be home before midnight. Carmen was out of town for a wedding. I stood dumbfounded in the middle of the hall, thinking, "What am I going to do? I don't want to call a locksmith, and worse, I'm not *dressed* to go anywhere. It was 7:00 pm and I wanted desperately to get my keys. I called my homegirl to let her know that I was coming to pick up her keys and headed to the party. I touched up my makeup and pulled the curls on my Afro. I totally forgot I was wearing the Elizabeth tee. I received so many compliments on my tee at the party! In fact, I met a freelance wardrobe stylist who was booked to do a photo shoot. We made an appointment for her to pull some of Sistahs' tees for her shoot. The party was really rocking, so I forgot about the keys and hung. When I got home and saw the keys on the table, I laughed at my accident. As I peeled out of my Elizabeth t-shirt, I thought, "Damn, this shirt does good?!" Effortless fashion welcomed anytime.

T-shirt recipe for Elizabeth—Simple Scoop Top

10 MINUTES WITH MACHINE
20 MINUTES BY HAND

- 1 T-SHIRT ANY SIZE
- HAND SEWING NEEDLES
- IRON
- IRONING BOARD
- SCISSORS
- SEAM RIPPER
- STRAIGHT PINS
- TAILOR'S CHALK
- TAPE MEASURE
- THIMBLE
- THREAD
- SEWING MACHINE (OPTIONAL)
- SEWING MACHINE NEEDLES (OPTIONAL)
- BOBBINS (OPTIONAL)

DIFFICULTY LEVEL • • 1 • • *Painless.*

No sewing experience required. You do not need to sew to make this shirt. You can sew it by hand in 20 minutes and by machine in 10 minutes. This shirt is a blast to make. It's a great project to get your feet wet. It's a quick, completely precious creation.

Simple Scoop Top

10 MINUTES WITH MACHINE • 20 MINUTES BY HAND

Step 1: Mark t-shirt with tailor's chalk see illustration below. Keep in mind your measurements per below. Save the remains from every t-shirt.

Step 2: Cut ½" around tailor's chalk line for seam allowance. For neck line, cut directly on scoop neck line. Also cut bottom hem from original t-shirt to make shoulder straps. Then cut twice for two pieces.

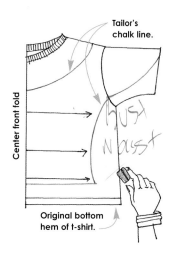

Tailor's chalk line.

Center front fold

Original bottom hem of t-shirt.

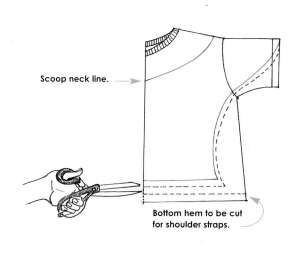

Scoop neck line.

Bottom hem to be cut for shoulder straps.

Step 3: Cut at center fold of sleeves, stopping at the original arm hole seams. This gives you sleeve slits.

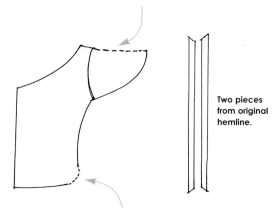

Two pieces from original hemline.

For extra girl flair, cut corners at bottom in a round shape. Follow cutting path in step #2 above.

Step 4: Pin to sew by hand or by machine. See illustration at right.

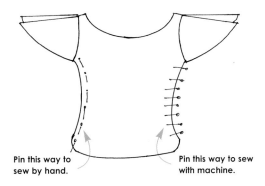

Pin this way to sew by hand.

Pin this way to sew with machine.

Step 5: For a more deconstructed look, you might want to see the stitch on the outside of the shirt. Therefore, do *not* turn the t-shirt inside out to sew it. Sew the correct side of the fabric. Sew side seams together with a top stitch.

For cute little side slits at bottom of shirt, stop your side seams about 2" above the bottom edge.

Step 6: Tie the straps at the shoulder.

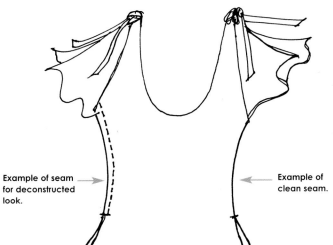

Example of seam for deconstructed look.

Example of clean seam.

Chapter 6

Theresa

Tie Front Athletic Top

A great t-shirt that is certainly *not* intended for basketball practice, this sassy athletic t-shirt wraps around the neck and around the waist. The extraordinary long neck sash allows for several styling options. It is feisty and eye catching.

I (Carmia) wore this style tee shirt to a De La Soul Concert at Central Park's Summer Stage. My friends and I were ready to jam, and we packed our food for the concert, daisies to share with other concert attendees, plenty of water, and a good spirit. I chose to wear the Theresa top. I love this style because it transitions into night garb well. We needed to stop by the store to pick up more orange juice for the concert. It was such a beautiful day that we didn't mind walking a few extra blocks to get what we needed for the day. I will admit, I was feeling rather attractive in my newly reworked tee. Every time I passed someone they would compliment me on my shirt. Rocking out at the concert, someone yelled, "I like your shirt." Heading to the subway, I heard, "Girl, you're wearing that shirt." I felt like I was in a movie.

Another time I wore this sassy athletic top just to stroll around Harlem with a girlfriend. I had on a pair of old jeans and flip-flops (not even high heels!). Compliments come again from every direction. Even an elderly woman shared her appreciation for such a special tee. My girlfriend and I continued our summer stroll, and when we finally made it to her house, before she let me into her apartment, she stared at me, her eyes as serious as if she were in a heated debate, and said, "I think you betta make me one of these shirts!" I laughed until my jaws hurt. After that, I promised myself to always wear it when I want an immense amount of attention.

T-shirt Recipe for Theresa—Tie Front Athletic Top

15 MINUTES WITH MACHINE
25 MINUTES BY HAND

- HOW LONG?
- 1 L OR XL T-SHIRT
- IRON
- IRONING BOARD
- SCISSORS
- SEAM RIPPER
- HAND SEWING NEEDLES
- STRAIGHT PINS
- TAILOR'S CHALK
- TAPE MEASURE
- THREAD
- SEWING MACHINE (OPTIONAL)
- BOBBINS (OPTIONAL)

DIFFICULTY LEVEL •• 2 •• *Easy.*

Wear a thimble and you're good to go. You'll be surprised how easy it is to make this shirt. Make sure when you're sewing the laces to the front of the shirt, that the wrong sides face you. By doing this, when you pull the laces up to tie around your neck, the correct side of the fabric will show. We tied the laces only one way in our photo. Use your imagination. One of the reasons the lace is so long is to give you five styling options. Make sure you take advantage of them.

Tie Front Athletic Top

15 MINUTES WITH MACHINE • 25 MINUTES BY HAND

Step 1: Using tailor's chalk, mark the shape as demonstrated in illustration below for the bodice. Keep in mind your measurements. Mark the straps; if the t-shirt is large enough, they should each be 3½" long.

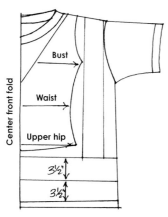

Step 2: Cut out bodice as well as straps. Look at the diagram below of perforated lines for your cutting path. Remember your ½''' seam allowance and cut directly on the marked line for V-neck and arm shape.

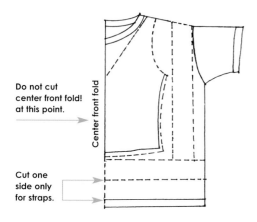

Step 3: If you are using a machine, place straps together then join by sewing ½" seam allowance. Look at diagram below. Take strap pieces and sew the ends together. Sew piece 1 to piece 3. Sew piece 2 to piece 4. If you sew by hand, overlap ends by ½". Then sew together. Look at diagram below.

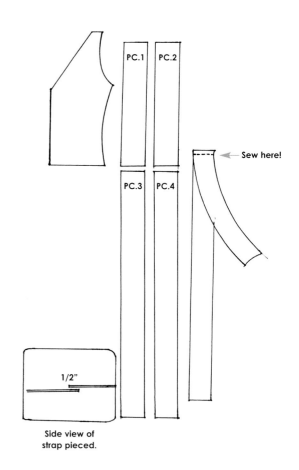

Side view of strap pieced.

Step 4: Pin, then sew side seams and straps onto bodice. **Note:** Be sure to sew straps with reversed side of fabric facing you, so that when turned upward, they are on the correct side of the fabric.

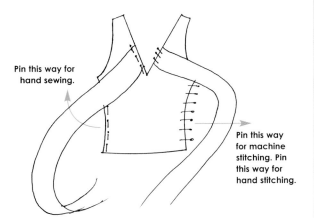

Pin this way for hand sewing.

Pin this way for machine stitching. Pin this way for hand stitching.

Chapter 7
Francesca

V-neck Corset Top

The Corset tee is a flirty V-neck and V-back tee with lace-up detail. The cool thing about this t-shirt is that it has a laid-back party vibe. Seems like an oxymoron, but this shirt reveals how dissimilar worlds can get along, for example the humble tee and a grand accessory like banging boots. If the tee is calm, spice it up with dramatic boots. Why not gain the best of both worlds? I (Carmen) made this shirt for my best friend. Clarisa was always complaining that she did not have anything to wear and wanted some more Sistah shirts. We were having dinner at her apartment, so I decided to hook her up and make her a t-shirt. I gently asked, "What style t-shirt would you like me to make you?" She knew this was a once in a life-time opportunity, so she went all out with her design. She begin describing "the shirt of her dreams." "Carmen, I want one with puff sleeves and a sash waist and with leather . . . . " The details were non-stop. I attentively listened, grabbed a napkin, and begin to sketch her design. She ran to her closet and brought me one of her favorite tees and a domestic sewing machine. I took a deep breath and I began to cut. Mid-production, Clarisa changed her mind. "I'm cutting your shirt, Clarisa, I can't change the design." Disappointed, Clarisa began to cry, sobbing about how much the tee meant to her. My girl was driving me crazy, but I cherish my friendship with her and could not leave her shirt unfinished. I took a deep breath and we re-designed the tee. And the Francesca corset tee was born. Despite the commotion, we created a splendid tee.

Also, V-neck t-shirts make me want to chunk up with accessories. It's an open space on the neck that calls for some attention. Besides, accessories add character to your look. Add a bold necklace for a cosmopolitan look.

T-Shirt Recipe for Francesca— V-neck Corset Top

30 MINUTES WITH MACHINE
45 MINUTES BY HAND

- 1 L OR XL T-SHIRT
- ¼" YARD OF LIGHTWEIGHT IRON-ON INTERFACING
- HAND SEWING NEEDLES
- IRON
- IRONING BOARD
- SEAM RIPPER
- SEWING MACHINE (OPTIONAL)
- BOBBINS (OPTIONAL)
- STRAIGHT PINS
- TAILOR'S CHALK
- TAPE MEASURE
- THREAD

DIFFICULTY LEVEL •• 4 •• Challenging.

You can't do it in an hour, but it can definitely be assembled. This is a hard shirt to make. Unlike some of the other styles, you have to have your game face on and you really have to pay attention to details. The lace detail in the back is tricky. It requires interfacing. When you purchase your interfacing, inquire about the various brands. Some brands adhere quicker than others.

V-neck Corset Top

30 MINUTES WITH MACHINE • 45 MINUTES BY HAND

Step 1: Mark t-shirt using tailor's chalk as shown in illustration (right).

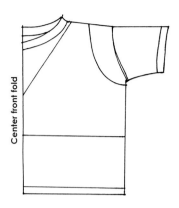

Step 2: Cut out bodice using cutting path in illustration. Be sure **not** to cut original side seams or shoulder seams.

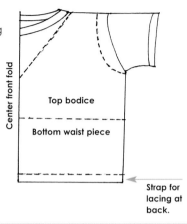

Top bodice

Bottom waist piece

Strap for lacing at back.

Step 3: Fold bottom waist piece overlapping each fold a ½". Then, with an iron, press these folds very well.

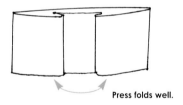

Press folds well.

Step 4: Turn bottom waist piece inside out and pull out flat; there will be indentations of the pressed folds. Cut two 1"-wide pieces of iron-on interfacing strips the same length as the bottom waist piece.

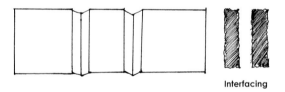

Interfacing

Step 5: Place the iron-on pieces of interfacing on the reversed side of bottom waist piece where the folds are. Then press them into place, using an iron. Various kinds of interfacing take different times to adhere to the fabric.

So when purchasing interfacing confirm the heat set time for the interfacing.

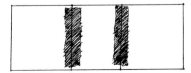

Step 6: Then turn the bottom waist back to its correct side. Then cut three very small slits into each fold. Be sure just to cut the actual fold and not the bottom back piece. Be careful to lift the actual fold that has the interfacing on the reverse side, then fold it in a ½" and cut three very small slits— only three.

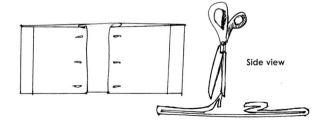

Side view

Step 7: Then sew a basting ½" above edge for top bodice. Then pull to get a gathered bottom edge. Remember not to pull too tight. Secure the end in a knot.

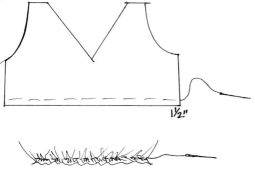

Step 8: Pin, then sew the top bodice to the bottom piece. Make sure that bottom piece is turned inside out for clean lines. You can have some fun and place the logo upside down as we did.

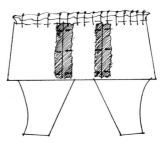

Step 9: Turn Corset Tee back onto its proper side, and using a strap pre-cut from the original hemline, lace it through back folded pieces through slits.

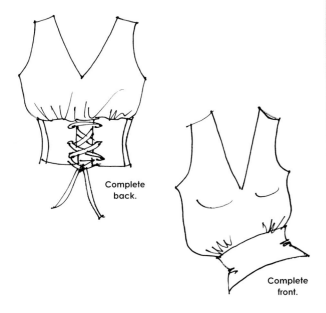

Complete back.

Complete front.

Chapter 8

Cuban Disco

One Shoulder Ruffle Top

Ruffled Rage! Fire up your femininity with ruffles. Let them conceal and reveal and fit you to a T. We love ruffles. We throw them on our shirts to give them a girly edge that is refreshing and upbeat.

The Cuban Disco top is a one-shoulder sensation with side ruffles that scream "show me to the dance floor." This baby is as sassy as it wants to be. We save this style tee for when we're ready to rock.

Here's a Sistah's style tip: hair adornments are timeless. A flower in your hair is *never* out of style. Add the flower of your choice for additional flava. If flowers aren't your thing, add semi-precious stones or other hair accessories that complement your new tee.

It's always about pumping up the positive and creating various dimensions to your T-robe. We love to dance. Music inspires us tremendously. We love to see this tee get down. Its side ruffles move—one, two, three, four, five, six without a problem. A lot of our friends are emerging musicians. We lend clothes and style upcoming artists for their showcases and performances around town. It's surreal to watch your garments come to life on a moving body, especially a dancing one!

Ali, a friend of ours, is an amazing singer and professional tap dancer. Her energy is sublimely volcanic. You feel her intensity and become affected by her performance. She wore the Cuban Disco to SOBs when performing with a Brazilian band. We were under a trance. Two loves, Ali and the Cuban Disco top, performing as one. It's wonderful when you envision an idea and it turns out to be a hotter tee than you imagined. The Cuban Disco top is a beauty and we'll watch Ali perform in it anytime.

T-Shirt Recipe for Cuban Disco—One Shoulder Ruffle Top

35 MINUTES
MUST HAVE MACHINE

- 1 L T-SHIRT
- ¼" ELASTIC (3–4 YARDS)
- HAND SEWING NEEDLES
- HEMMING TAPE
- IRON
- IRONING BOARD
- MACHINE NEEDLES
- SEAM RIPPER
- SEWING MACHINE REQUIRED
- BOBBINS
- STRAIGHT PINS
- TAILOR'S CHALK
- THIMBLE
- THREAD

DIFFICULTY LEVEL ●● 4 ●● *Challenging.*

Be prepared to spend some time with your couture tee. This is a tough shirt. Sewing the elastic is not easy. You need a steady hand, especially if you're using a sewing machine. This shirt has clean seams with a ruffle. Tricky. After you cut out the shirt, reverse the shirt so both sides of the fabric are face to face. When you sew your seams together, however, your ruffles are between front and back. **Practice sewing elastic to a piece of scrap fabric first. This is difficult to do, but not impossible!**

One Shoulder Ruffle Top

35 MINUTES • MUST HAVE MACHINE

Step 1: Using tailor's chalk, mark the basic shape that's shown in illustration below.

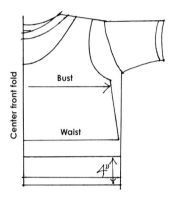

Step 2: Cut out shapes using cutting path as shown in illustration below.

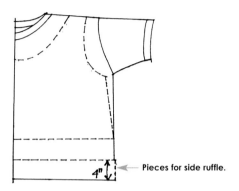

Step 3: Open the bodice of the t-shirt, then cut again across the top edge using this cutting path.

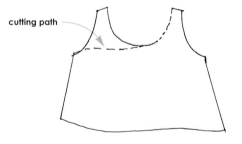

Step 4: Take your two pieces for side ruffles and do your basting stitch. Then pull thread through basting stitch with a drawstring method. The distance between basting stitch and top edge is ½" only.

(**NOTE**: THE LENGTH OF THE RUFFLES SHOULD BE SIDE SEAM MEASUREMENT MINUS 2")

Step 5: Turn shirt inside out, secure side ruffles inside facing the correct side of bodice with straight pins. Then sew side-seams using ½" seam allowance. Remember there should be 2" at bottom hem for the elastic waistband to be sewn in.

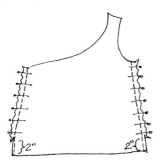

Step 6: Make 2 elastic bands ¼" or ½". It is your choice. Cut one elastic band 3" less than your waist measurements. Then cut the other elastic band 2" less than your bust measurements.

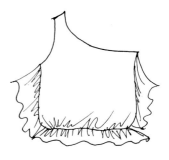

Step 7: PRACTICE SEWING ELASTIC TO A PIECE OF SCRAP FABRIC FIRST. THIS IS DIFFICULT TO DO, BUT NOT IMPOSSIBLE! Be sure to pin the ruffles up and away from the bottom line of the bodice so you do not accidentally sew the elastic over the hem.

A Place elastic at side seam. Do not pull elastic yet. Make a secure stitch about ¼" long. Refer to glossary for secure stitching.

B Then proceed to sew exactly down the middle of the elastic. At this point, pull the elastic with one hand and guide through the machine with the other hand. Try not to pull too tight.

C Then repeat the same process at the new neckline you've cut out. This time only give ¼" seam allowance.

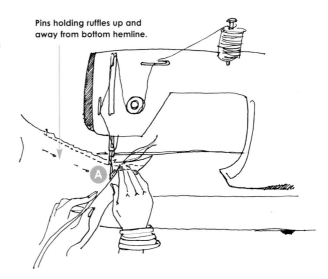

Pins holding ruffles up and away from bottom hemline.

Step 8: Take out all the pins. Then turn your shirt onto the correct side. And there you have it—ready to go.

Chapter 9

Cairo

Double Ruffle V-neck Delight Top

The Cairo shirt, sweet and easy, has a raw edge V-neck and double-ruffled sleeve. Great for the girl who requires only 15 minutes of mirror time.

Pictured in Kelly green, we encourage you to use bright colored t-shirts. Intense colors make the ruffles pop. This style transitions well into any atmosphere. "Take me to the park, to dinner, to a movie, or to a concert."

Ruffles are a girl's best friend. We throw them on our shirts to give them a frilly edge that's refreshing and youthful. I (Carmen) love wearing the Cairo style when I want to feel flirty. I subtly shake my ruffles at a cutie on the subway.

This shirt is so fun and light. The cool thing about this t-shirt is that you can wear it in the Fall. Add a solid colored tee underneath the Cairo style. You have a really cute layered look.

DIFFICULTY LEVEL •• 2 •• *Easy, almost breezy.*

A little concentration is necessary. Another easy creation. However, be careful when pinning your ruffles. You want to make sure that they are far enough apart to create a tiered ruffle on your shoulders as pictured.

T-shirt recipe for Cairo—Double Ruffle V-neck Delight Top

20 MINUTES WITH MACHINE
35 MINUTES BY HAND

- ONE SHOULDER RUFFLE TOP
- 1 T-SHIRT, ANY SIZE
- HAND SEWING NEEDLES
- IRON
- IRONING BOARD
- SCISSORS
- SEAM RIPPER
- SEWING MACHINE (OPTIONAL)
- SEWING MACHINE NEEDLES (OPTIONAL)
- BOBBINS (OPTIONAL)
- STRAIGHT PINS
- TAPE MEASURE
- THIMBLE
- THREAD

Double Ruffle V-neck Delight Top

20 MINUTES WITH MACHINE • 35 MINUTES BY HAND

Step 1: Mark shape as shown in illustration below with tailor's chalk.

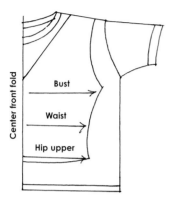

Step 2: Cut shapes out using cutting path in illustration below as your guide. You should have 5 pieces to work with.

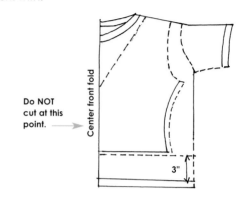

Step 3:

A Take the sleeves and bottom remains of the t-shirt and sew a basting stitch 1" from the raw edges cut.

B Then pull your thread in a drawstring manner through the basting stitch you've made previously. Remember, do not pull too tight.

NOTE: THIS CAP SLEEVE SHOULD BE SAME LENGTH AS ARM HOLE.

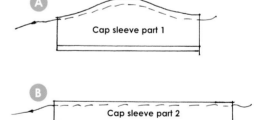

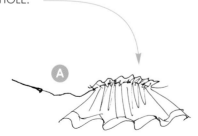

NOTE: THIS CAP SLEEVE CAN BE 2" SHORTER THAN RUFFLED SLEEVE PART 1 shown in illustration below.

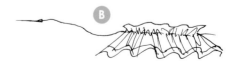

Step 4: See illustration below. Pin ruffled cap sleeves part 1 to the t-shirt. Make sure that the t-shirt is open and completely flat for easy sewing. Repeat on the opposite side. Then sew them onto shirt.

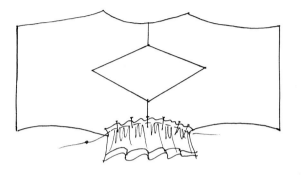

Step 5: Pin cap sleeves part 2 on top of part 1 which you have already secured. Then sew into place.

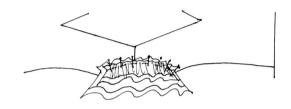

Step 6: Then once sleeves are securely sewn in place, sew side seams together and voila, your cute sassy tee is complete.

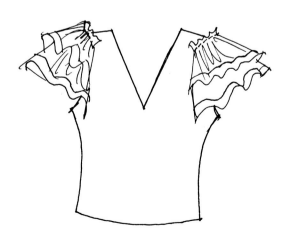

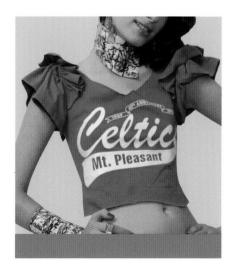

Chapter 10

Bella

Deep V-neck Top
with Removable Ruffle

Will it slide off or not? Keep 'em guessing with this most seductive style of t-shirt dressing. The Bella top embodies the adventure of a hot summer day (or night!). With a raw edge V-neck, snap tape, and removable ruffle, it's a ray of light. Its versatility is amazing. Once you make this tee, you will have two-in-one. Wear the ruffle to play. Lose the ruffle to entice.

Anniversary season knocked on my (Carmia) sister's door last summer. It was time to celebrate a successful one year of marriage. The couple decided to vacation on the Island of Jamaica. Wardrobe is always an issue when you take a special trip. You want to bring your entire closet but it's just not possible. My sister was calling this her second honeymoon and she wanted this getaway to be as exciting as their first honeymoon. Of course, she needed a tee. I had to hook her up. She wanted a festive t-shirt. I showed her the Bella top. She loved it. Not only was it energetic and contempo, but it was also multi-functional. I told her to wear the ruffle for brunch. For nighttime play, remove it. She smiled. Mission accomplished.

A whole t-shirt and a bottom half are required for this style. We highly recommend using a full t-shirt in a solid color for the bodice, and a half shirt with some pattern for the ruffle. Use any color snap tape you desire. We chose a canary yellow tee for the bodice, red snap tape, and a purple printed tee for the ruffle of our Bella top. (Be sure to wash red snap tape before using. Red tends to bleed.)

A lot is going down with this tee. Choose complementary colors to highlight all of the details. Go for gusto. The Bella top is ready to move!

T-shirt recipe for Bella—Deep V-neck Top with Removable Ruffle

35 MINUTES WITH MACHINE
45 MINUTES BY HAND

- 2 T-SHIRTS:
  1 L OR XL T-SHIRT (SOLID) &
  1 M OR L T-SHIRT (PRINTED)
- ALEENE'S FABRIC GLUE
- HAND SEWING NEEDLES
- IRON
- IRONING BROAD
- SCISSORS
- SEAM RIPPER
- SEWING MACHINE (OPTIONAL)
- SEWING MACHINE NEEDLES (OPTIONAL)
- BOBBINS
- SNAP TAPE (1 YARD)
- STRAIGHT PINS
- TAILOR'S CHALK
- TAPE MEASURE
- THREAD

DIFFICULTY LEVEL •• 4 •• Challenging.

Great things require great time. Sewing snap tape requires a steady hand.
A quick cheat - glue the snap tape with fabric glue to the t-shirt before sewing.
Allow to dry then stitch away.

Deep V-neck Corset Top With Removable Ruffle

30 MINUTES WITH MACHINE • 45 MINUTES BY HAND

Step 1: **First T-shirt (a solid color)** First, cut front of t-shirt apart from back! Then fold in half. Save the back part of t-shirt for step 5.

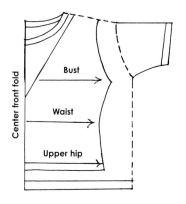

Step 2: **First T-shirt (a solid color)** Then cut out front using the cutting path shown in illustration below. Remember, seam allowance should be ½".

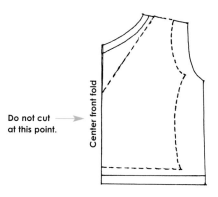

Step 3: **Second T-shirt (printed t-shirt)** Cut (2) 4"-wide pieces from your printed shirt or t-shirt. Be sure to cut pieces where the print or image falls on the shirt.

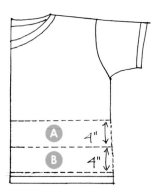

Step 4: Make a basting stitch ¼" from top line of piece. Then pull through with a drawstring action. DO NOT PULL TOO TIGHT. (REMEMBER, THIS MUST BE SEWN ONTO THE SNAP TAPE.)

Then sew these two pieces together to make one long piece.

Step 5: **First T-shirt (solid)** For the back piece of first t-shirt, take the back piece, and fold in half. Lay your pre-cut from bodice piece on top. Then trace using tailor's chalk (the arm hole, side, and bottom only). You will change the neckline, using crewneck t-shirt for the right shape.

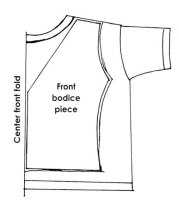

Step 6: Then cut out your back piece using this cutting path.

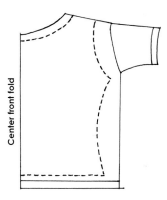

Step 7: Sew front bodice to back. Remember to place correct side facing each other. (ONLY SEW THE SHOULDER SEAMS FOR NOW!) Do not sew side seams yet.

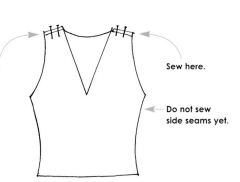

Deep V-neck Corset Top With Removable Ruffle

30 MINUTES WITH MACHINE • 45 MINUTES BY HAND

Step 8: Then turn top onto the correct side as shown here. Then use fabric glue to attach snap tape to the top as well as the long ruffle piece. Aleene's fabric glue is the perfect choice. Allow it at least 10 minutes to dry. Make sure you measure snap tape pieces to make sure they match perfectly. We suggest snapping it together before you cut it.

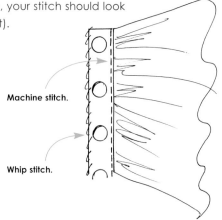

Step 9: Sew your ruffle piece with the glued snap tape. If you are using a sewing machine, we suggest you use a zipper foot. Also sew your bodice with glued snap tape using the same zipper foot for ease when passing the metal or plastic snaps. NOTE: IF YOU ARE SEWING BY HAND USE A WHIP STITCH. If using a machine, your stitch should look like illustration (right).

Machine stitch.

Whip stitch.

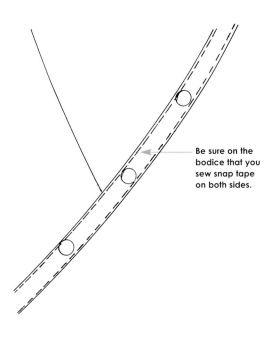

Be sure on the bodice that you sew snap tape on both sides.

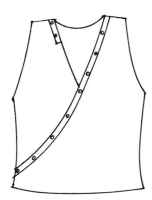

Step 10: Sew your side seams together. It is your choice whether to sew a top stitch exposing deconstructed edges or to turn it inside out and sew a proper clean finish seam. The great thing is that you have two looks in one t-shirt. One very simple rocker girl with just the snap tape and the other free, flirty ruffles!

Chapter 11

Miami

Multi-colored Bikini Top

Diva Tees. Stop the press! If you're wearing this shirt, the stage is yours! This t-shirt bikini top is ready for tanning on the beach or the electricity of a sizzling celebration. If you want to flaunt your abs, this shirt will do it. You've been in the gym all winter, now work those abs, girl!!

The Miami tee is magnetic for all the right reasons. When creating the Miami tee, you want to use a variety of complementary colored t-shirts and an athletic jersey. Our Miami top, demonstrated in fuchsia, yellow, teal, and green is a combo of vibrant colors. You will have more than usual t-shirt remains with this style. Don't consider it wasteful. Save the scraps. You can use them for other t-shirt styles. The Miami tee is great for an outdoor adventure.

It's also a great layering piece. Throw this bikini top over a solid color tee for an extra dimension to your ensemble. You can also wear it underneath other shirts, blazers, and denim jackets. Truly, this tee is da bomb!

DIFFICULTY LEVEL •• 2 •• *Smooth sailing.*

You barely have to lift a finger to make this fly tee. The most challenging part is finding complementary colors that flatter you.

T-shirt Recipe for Miami—Multi-colored Bikini Top

20 MINUTES WITH MACHINE
30 MINUTES BY HAND

- 2 T-SHIRTS ANY SIZE
- 1 V-NECK JERSEY X OR XL
- HAND SEWING NEEDLES
- IRON
- IRONING BOARD
- SCISSORS
- SEAM RIPPER
- SEWING MACHINE (OPTIONAL)
- SEWING MACHINE NEEDLES (OPTIONAL)
- BOBBINS (OPTIONAL)
- STRAIGHT PINS
- TAILOR'S CHALK
- TAPE MEASURE
- THREAD

Multi-colored Bikini Top

20 MINUTES WITH MACHINE • 30 MINUTES BY HAND

Step 1: **For your first t-shirt** cut the hem off at 3½" wide; you will have 2 pieces.

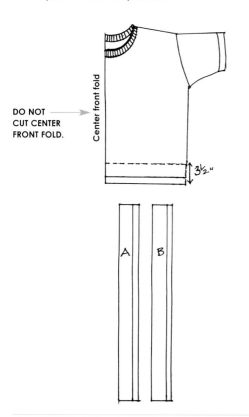

DO NOT CUT CENTER FRONT FOLD.

Center front fold

3½"

A   B

Step 2: **For your second t-shirt,** follow cutting path in illustration below. For measurements Exhibit **C**, it should be ¼" of your bust measurement.

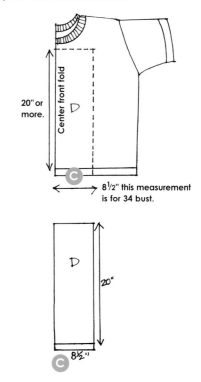

20" or more.

Center front fold

D

C 8½" this measurement is for 34 bust.

D

20"

C 8½"

Step 3: To achieve the exact same look as our bikini top, you will need a great athletic tape trim, V-neck. Remember do not cut side shoulder seam. It should have the same measurements as your previous step 2 piece.

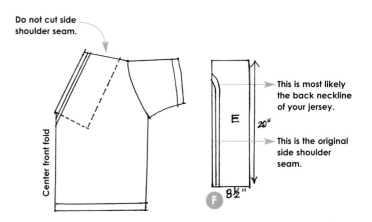

Do not cut side shoulder seam.

Center front fold

E   20"

This is most likely the back neckline of your jersey.

This is the original side shoulder seam.

F 8½"

Step 4: Take your pieces **A** & **B** and sew the ends together. Regard the illustrations.

Step 5: Take your piece **D** & **E** and cut as follows; Pay attention to the measurements. **D** & **E** are different because Piece **D** is on the center fold!

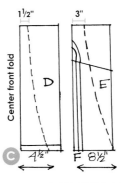

Step 6: Then take **D** & **E** pin them to **A** & **B**. Remember unfold piece **D** so that it will be 8½" wide at the **C** edge line.

Also more important, turn pieces **E** & **D** over so that the correct sides face each other. After you turn over piece **E**, pin then sew. Stitching path is highlighted here. Previously sewn piece, fold upward out of the way, so that you can pin and sew piece **D**. Again, sewing path is highlighted. Once all pieces are sewn together you will have a funny almost "x" shape look at step 6 above. So when you put it on and pull it, the halter will fall into place.

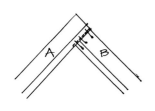

Bikini pieces unfolded

After you turn over piece E, pin then sew. Stitching path is highlighted here.

Previously sewn piece, fold upward out of the way, so that you can pin and sew piece D. Again, sewing path is highlighted.

Chapter 12
Kyoko

Extravagant Sash Top

Draping glory! The Kyoko t-shirt is a gathered halter with a bold neck ribbon and waist sash. Say sayonara to your old halters. Indeed, a club banger showstopper! This shirt is blazing. Sleek. Sexy. Hands down, this tee says, "Hello, I know you're looking!" Whiplash is no stranger.

This tee has an avant-garde appeal, a street funk punk look. It sashays through any hip environs freely and unapologetically.

Bunch it together for that fun twist on elegance. The end result is sizzling off the meter. This is one of my (Carmia) favorite styles in the book. I wear this shirt when I want to impress someone with a kickin', flat out, phenomenal tee. Once, a man glanced over at me as we both viewed the Basquiat exhibit at the Brooklyn Museum of Art, and said, "Your shirt should be on display." I was beyond flattered!

DIFFICULTY LEVEL •• 3 •• *Sewing 101 is useful.*

Looks harder than it is. Note: Use an extremely oversized t-shirt for this style. The Kyoko tee gathers in the front so the larger size is essential for draping.

T-shirt recipe for Kyoko—Extravagant Sash Top

15 MINUTES WITH MACHINE
25 MINUTES BY HAND

- 1 XL T-SHIRT
- HAND SEWING NEEDLES
- IRON
- IRONING BOARD
- SEWING MACHINE (OPTIONAL)
- BOBBINS (OPTIONAL)
- STRAIGHT PINS
- TAILOR'S CHALK
- TAPE MEASURE
- THREAD

Extravagant Sash Top

15 MINUTES WITH MACHINE • 25 MINUTES BY HAND

Step 1: Start with the back of the original t-shirt facing you. Then cut straight down the center back—ONLY cut the center back. Leave the front completely intact. Also, cut the sleeves off using a raglan sleeve line as shown in the cutting in illustration below.

Step 2: Open the cut t-shirt to its reversed side. Then cut the entire original ribbed crewneck off. Proceed to sew the pre-cut arm holes together as shown below. Sew **A** to **B**, as shown in illustration below. Save the remains; you will need the sleeves.

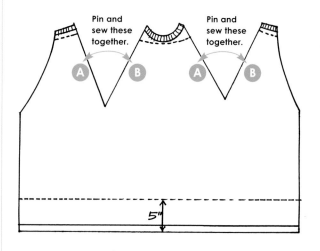

Step 3: Cut waste sash from bottom of original hemline. Make sure it's 5" wide.

Step 4: Make a basting stitch at the top neckline 1" from top edge.

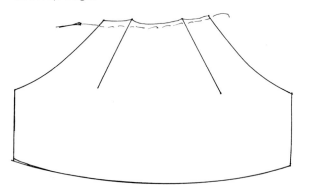

Step 5: Cut 3 pieces from one of the remaining sleeve pieces. One piece will be the neck ribbon at 2½" wide. The other 2 pieces will be the belt loop straps. See illustration below.

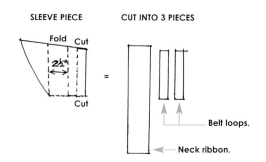

Step 6: Pull your basting through like a drawstring. Then sew across the same stitch to secure the gathering. Then sew the belt loops at the sides.

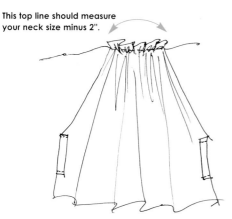

This top line should measure your neck size minus 2".

Step 7: Pull neck ribbon a bit to stretch it. Then sew it on top of the gathered neckline, leaving a 1" space to the top edge.

Step 8: Pull the 5" waist sash through belt loops on the sides, and it's absolutely smashing.

Chapter 13

Margarita

Runched Sensation Top

A splash of hot color doesn't hurt any t-shirt. With its gathered center seam and hot colored neck sash, the playful Margarita top is ideal for the bold girl full of fun and adventure. This style makes us want to go to the beach, lay out on the sand and watch the sun disappear behind the coastline. And no, you're not limited to hot pants with this look. A long flowing A-line skirt is equally complementary. It's your choice. Either way, you're going to look wonderful!

When choosing the neck sash for the Margarita tee, we recommend using a bright or bold color. It's one of the many dynamic elements of the t-shirt. Surprise the masses with an unexpected contrasting color in the center of your reworked tee.

It's also a fun opportunity to deconstruct a familiar logo on a basic tee, splitting it right down the center.

DIFFICULTY LEVEL • • 5 • • Intense.

Several steps are required to make this shirt. It's the small details of this project that can throw you off. We sew elastic to create the runched center front. It's a great look; however, it's complicated to create. Sewing elastic can be tough. Practice sewing elastic onto a scrap of fabric first, to avoid making mistakes on the real deal. Move slowly and steadily, and you'll succeed with flying colors.

T-shirt Recipe for Margarita— Runched Sensation Top

60 MINUTES WITH MACHINE SEWING MACHINE REQUIRED

- ¼" ELASTIC (1 YD)
- 2 XL T-SHIRTS
- HAND SEWING NEEDLES
- IRON
- IRONING BOARD
- SCISSORS
- SEAM RIPPER
- SEWING MACHINE NEEDLES
- TAILOR'S CHALK
- TAPE MEASURE
- THREAD

Runched Sensation Top

60 MINUTES WITH MACHINE • SEWING MACHINE REQUIRED

Step 1: **First t-shirt** Cut front piece away from the back. Save that back piece for the next step. This step is demonstrated in red. Then cut rectangular pieces from the pre-cut front bodice, and follow the cutting path marked in black. You will have two front pieces when you finish cutting.

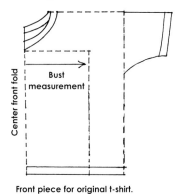

Front piece for original t-shirt.

Step 2: Take pre-cut back piece of t-shirt and fold it in half. Then cut as shown in illustration below. Make sure it is the same length as the front piece. Your back piece should be ½" wider than your front piece.

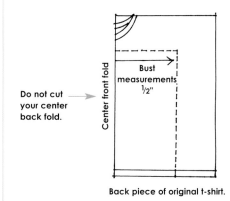

Back piece of original t-shirt.

Step 3: **Second t-shirt** Your second t-shirt will be the halter neck piece for this style. Use a bright complementary color. As with the previous t-shirt, cut the front panel away from the back as shown in illustration below in red. Then fold that front piece in half as shown. Proceed to cut out your neck piece using the cutting path shown in illustration below. Remember to regard your measurements as illustrated.

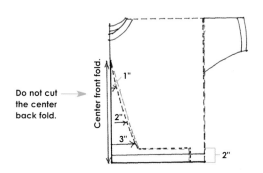

Step 4: Take your two front pre-cut pieces and pin together for cutting. Then take your pre-cut halter neck piece and lay it over the front pieces, as shown in illustration **A**. Mark tailor's chalk along the outside of the neck halter piece. After you mark it, remove the neck halter piece and cut along the line that you marked, as shown in illustration **B**.

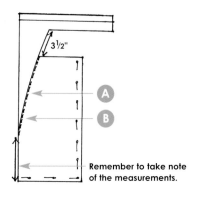

Remember to take note of the measurements.

Step 5: Now open your neck halter piece. Pin, then sew your two front pieces to the neck halter piece. Do one side at a time. See illustration. Once you have sewn both front pieces to the neck halter, sew the remaining center front edges together. They are high-lighted in illustration **A**. Turn this piece over, then pin and sew it to the neck halter piece. Repeat this process on the other side. See illustration **B**. Your front piece should look like illustration **C** when you have completed sewing all three pieces together.

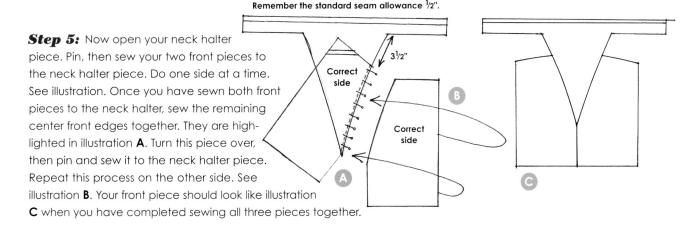

Correct side

3¹/₂"

Correct side

B

A

C

Step 6: Practice this next step on scrap pieces of fabric before proceeding. Sew two ¹/₄"-wide elastic bands to reverse side of the front bodice. After you reverse your front bodice piece, measure the distance between **A** and **C**. Your elastic bands should be 3" less than that measurement. Secure a stitch 1" into the elastic at point **A**. You will use the same pull and guide technique from Chapter 7. Guide and hold the elastic in one hand and pull with the other hand. Repeat the same technique for points **D** to **F**. (MAKE SURE THAT YOU FOLLOW THE SEWING PATH HIGHLIGHTED IN GREEN.)

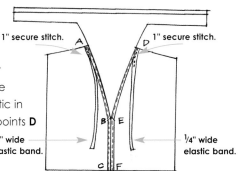

1" secure stitch.   1" secure stitch.

¹/₄" wide elastic band.   ¹/₄" wide elastic band.

A   D
B   E
C   F

Step 7: Now take the back bodice piece which is ¹/₂" wider on each side. Turn it around so that the correct side of fabric faces the front bodice piece. **A** should line up with **B**, and **C** with **D**. Then pin and sew the side seams together. You will have to pull sides **B** and **D** downward to match up with points **A** and **C**.

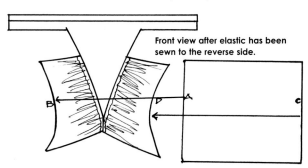

Front view after elastic has been sewn to the reverse side.

B   D   A   C

Step 8: This is your top inside out after the back panel is sewn down both side seams. Simply turn it onto its correct side, slip it on, and tie it at the neck.

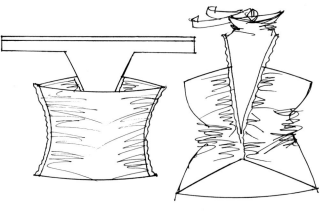

Chapter 14
Daddy Bruce

Tuxedo Top

Indeed, grandpa has style. This deconstructed halter has a necktie attached to the collar. This style mixes business with pleasure. The girl who wears this style tee is a mover and a shaker. She has places to go and people to see, networking to do and meetings to attend. Like herself, her garments are multifaceted. The Daddy Bruce has a mature quality, yet it does not forsake style. An all-time favorite, its design is strong and timeless.

I (Carmen) have been wearing this style for years. Every time I try to remove the Daddy Bruce tee from my closet, I can't. I wear it and I get rave reviews. Here, pictured in blue with maroon and black, gray, and white stripes, we tied the necktie in an ascot style. We love this. Please wear it this way. However, you are not limited to this option. You can change the tie as you please. Try a four in hand tie knot to the front or to the back. Variety is awesome.

DIFFICULTY LEVEL ·· 5 ·· *Complex.*

Red Bull vital. You must have a sewing machine for this style.

T-shirt Recipe for Daddy Bruce— Tuxedo Top

40 MINUTES WITH MACHINE
SEWING MACHINE REQUIRED

- 1 L T-SHIRT
- 1 MEN'S NECK TIE
- HAND SEWING NEEDLES
- IRON
- IRONING BOARD
- SCISSORS
- SEAM RIPPER
- SEWING MACHINE NEEDLES
- SEWING MACHINE REQUIRED
- BOBBINS
- STRAIGHT PINS
- TAILOR'S CHALK
- TAPE MEASURE
- THREAD

Tuxedo Top

40 MINUTES WITH MACHINE • SEWING MACHINE REQUIRED

Step 1: You must have an extra large t-shirt for his style. First cut the front panel from the back using the cutting path shown in illustration below. Then use tailor's chalk to mark your shape as shown. Then proceed to cut. You will have 5 pieces.

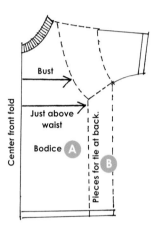

Step 2: Once you have cut out the basic bodice shape and 2 pieces for back ties, begin to fold and press cummerbund-like pleats, moving in an upward direction. You should be able to get five pleats. You can use hemming tape or straight pins to hold the pleats in place.

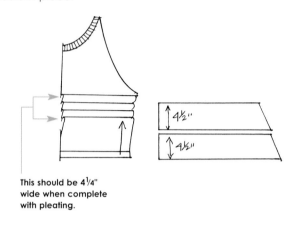

This should be 4¼" wide when complete with pleating.

Step 3: Once you have secured your pleats with hemming tape or straight pins, then sew the pleats down using a top stitch. Your stitches should be as close as possible to the edge of each pleat. Approximately ½" if possible.

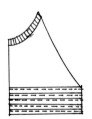

Step 4: Once you have completed the top stitching on each pleat, sew both back sash ties to the sides. Remember to sew using a clean and invisible stitch method, placing correct sides facing each other. See illustration below.

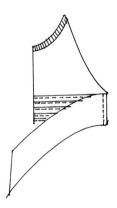

Step 5: Once you have sewn the back ties at the side bodice, fold over and press. Be sure that you have a ¼" overlap. Then sew a topstitch to secure it.

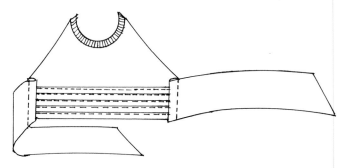

Step 6: Pin your men's tie of choice to the neck line of the halter (We recommend nice fat ties. The skinny ties from the 60s did not offer enough surface to work with.) Pin the tie onto the halter at the bottom of the crew neck. See illustration **A**. After pinning and sewing, use a topstitch to attach the tie to the halter at the bottom of the crewneck. Then remove pins and fold tie in an upward motion, revealing the correct side. Sew a rectangle shape onto crewneck. See illustration **B**.

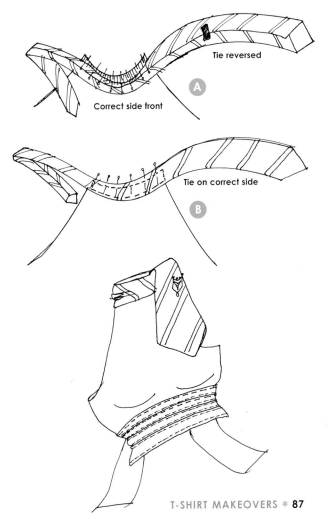

Chapter 15
Pocahontas

Braided Triumph Halter

Beautiful braid (from t-shirt scraps!) ties around the back of the neck. The Pocahontas shirt has an adorable halter that you can wear two ways. Shoulders are exposed, but rightfully so! We are wild about this shirt. Depending on your mood, you can let the braids from the tee hang on your shoulders for a carefree look or tie them to the back for a more refined look. It's another one of those tees that has major range.

Accessorize with bracelets. Wear them by the hundreds. Stack them on. It's a good look on bare arms!

Wear this tee wherever you want to go or *not* go. Whose says you can't enjoy your beauty in the comfort of your home?

DIFFICULTY LEVEL ● ● 3 ● ● *Sewing 101 is useful.*

Time consuming but not hard. Play your favorite song. Follow the instructions. You'll past the task with flying colors.

T-shirt Recipe for Pocahontas— Braided Triumph Halter

30 MINUTES WITH MACHINE
40 MINUTES BY HAND

- 1 M OR L T-SHIRT
- HAND SEWING NEEDLES
- IRON
- IRONING BOARD
- SCISSORS
- SEAM RIPPER
- SEWING MACHINE (OPTIONAL)
- SEWING MACHINE NEEDLES (OPTIONAL)
- BOBBINS (OPTIONAL)
- STRAIGHT PINS
- TAILOR'S CHALK
- TAPE MEASURE
- THREAD

Braided Triumph Halter

30 MINUTES WITH MACHINE • 40 MINUTES BY HAND

Step 1: Using the tailor's chalk, mark the shape of the bodice as shown in illustration below. It is very important to save all remains from this t-shirt because the scraps are used for braiding. Follow the cutting path in illustration below. Use all of the 1½" straps for braiding. You should have 13 pieces when you are done cutting.

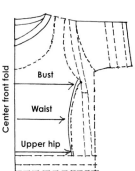

Step 2: Separate the back from the front piece and cut following the cutting path shown in illustration **A**. Then fold top of strap by one inch and sew them down. See article **A** shown in illustration.

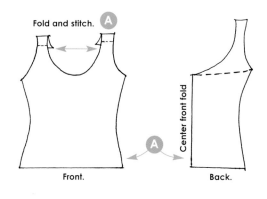

Fold and stitch. **A**

Front.

Back.

Center front fold

Step 3: Sew the back piece to the front piece. Choose a top stitch for a deconstructed look or stitch a clean traditional seam.

Step 4: Cut very small slits into the straps of the top. Make sure you stay within the folded stitch down the surface.

Small slits.

Back.

Step 5: Take 12 of the 13 pieces, then 2 short strips. Secure 3 strips by sewing a stitch at one end before braiding. Then braid your three strips together. Now you should have one long braided strip and 2 short ones. At the end of all braids, secure topstitching.

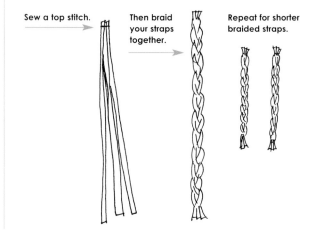

Sew a top stitch.

Then braid your straps together.

Repeat for shorter braided straps.

Step 6: Pull pre-braided strips at each end so that they are slimmer and tighter. Then pull the longer braided strip through the slits on the front bodice. Then take your smaller braided strips and tie them onto lone strip. These are two options for different looks.

Look 1
For a deeper, plunging scoop neck

Front.

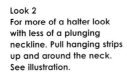

Look 2
For more of a halter look with less of a plunging neckline. Pull hanging strips up and around the neck. See illustration.

Back.

Chapter 16

Vintage Remix

Halter Top with Scarf

Mixing the old with the new is always F&F: fierce and fab! The Vintage Remix halter top can be worn on any occasion. This deconstructed halter has an attached scarf around the neck. The girl who sports this style is spicy during the day and on fire at night.

For casual day, wear a blazer and jeans for an urbane foxy look. For funky Saturday fun, lose the blazer. That's it. Burden-free. The Vintage Remix transforms into a hot, backless party t-shirt with scarf that can be tied any way you like.

Style Forecast: Razzle-dazzle, over-the-top belts are celebrity status! Add one for extra drama. Less is not always more.

DIFFICULTY LEVEL • • 5 • • *Complex.*

A rigorous sewing project; you'll need a nap before the soirée.

T-shirt Recipe for Vintage Remix— Halter Top with Scarf

40 MINUTES WITH MACHINE
SEWING MACHINE REQUIRED

- 1 M OR L T-SHIRT
- 1 VINTAGE SILK SCARF
- HAND SEWING NEEDLES
- MACHINE SEWING NEEDLES
- SCISSORS
- SEAM RIPPER
- SEWING MACHINE REQUIRED
- SEWING NEEDLES
- BOBBINS
- STRAIGHT PINS
- TAILOR'S CHALK
- TAPE MEASURE
- THREAD

Halter Top with Scarf

40 MINUTES WITH MACHINE • SEWING MACHINE REQUIRED?

Step 1: You must have an extra large t-shirt for this style. First cut from front panel from back using the cutting path shown in illustration below. Then use tailor's chalk to mark your shape as shown. Then proceed to cut. You will have five pieces.

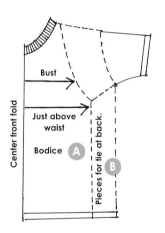

Step 2: Once you have cut out the basic bodice shape and 2 pieces for back ties, begin to fold and press cummerbund -ike pleats, moving in an upward direction. You should be able to get five pleats. You can use hemming tape or straight pins to hold the pleats in place.

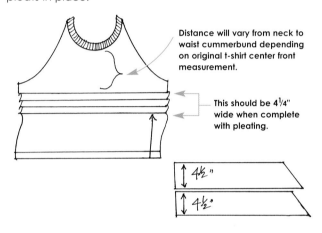

Step 3: Once you have secured your pleats with hemming tape or straight pins, sew the pleats down using a top stitch. Your stitches should be as close as possible to the edge of each pleat. Approxiamately ⅛" if possible.

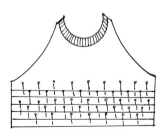

Note: pin pleats of the cummerbund before sewing them down.

Step 4: Then once you have completed sewing all top stitching on each pleat, proceed to sew both back sash ties to the sides. Remember to sew using a clean and invisible stitch method by placing correct sides facing each other. See illustration below.

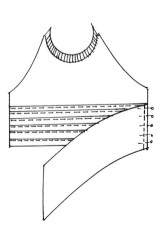

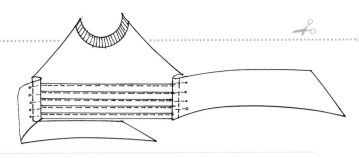

Step 5: Once you have sewn the back ties at the side seams, fold over and press. Be sure that you have a ¼" overlap. Then sew a topstitch to secure it.

Step 6: Use silk, rayon, or even polyester if you chose for the neck tie. Be sure to use a fairly large scarf. First, prep your scarf as follows: make a 3-step fold. Then sew the larger edges of the scarf to secure it.

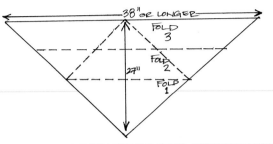

Step 7: Then lay scarf at bottom edge of original t-shirt crewneck and pin. Sew the scarf to the crewneck.

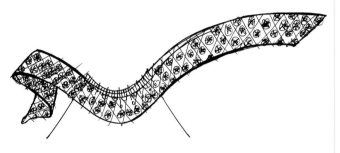

Step 8: After securing silk scarf onto crewneck with topstitch, just fold scarf upward and tie in the back of neck; or, as we have shown, tie at the side of the neck for elegance.

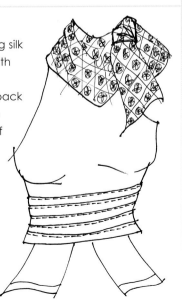

Chapter 17

Haile

Ritzy Wave Top

The sleeveless Haile top has a classic crewneck with ruffles and paillettes accenting the shoulder. Paillettes (pronounced pi-yettes) are pieces of glittery (BLINGING) materials used to adorn your tees, i.e. sequins. You can also use rhinestones, crystals, antique buttons, and jewels to jazz up your nerw creation. Ladies who adore this style embrace sporty elegance. For sophistication, wear black slacks and a black pump. For a funky Saturday night, lose the slacks. Add a mini skirt and a fun pair of sandals or combat boots, and you're ready for a night of excitement!

It's all about tees that can move from night to day. Sometimes we don't have the luxury of going home after work or school to make a complete change. I (Carmia) can remember numerous times when I needed to move quickly from casual to over-the-top! The Haile top helped to complete this task. With this shirt, in some cases, I don't even need to change my pants. I simply throw on a heeled pair of shoes (which I can fit in my purse) and I'm ready to rock out.

DIFFICULTY LEVEL ● ● 2 ● ● Lightweight.

The haile top is super easy to make. Make sure when creating your ruffles you don't pull the ruffles too tight. You want nice full ruffles, not tight puckered ruffles. Also, add your embellishments to the ruffles of your shirt last. We recommend that you do not add the embellishments until after the side seams have been sewn together. By doing this you eliminate the chances of displacing your embellishments. No details will get lost in the ruffle.

T-shirt recipe for Haile— Ritzy Wave Top

20 MINUTES WITH MACHINE
30 MINUTES BY HAND

- 1 T-SHIRT ANY SIZE
- HAND SEWING NEEDLES
- IRON
- IRONING BOARD
- PAILLETTES OR SEQUINS (OPTIONAL)
- SCISSORS
- SEWING MACHINE (OPTIONAL)
- SEWING MACHINE NEEDLES (OPTIONAL)
- BOBBINS (OPTIONAL)
- STRAIGHT PINS
- TAILOR'S CHALK
- TAPE MEASURE
- THIMBLE
- THREAD

Ritzy Wave Top

20 MINUTES WITH MACHINE • 30 MINUTES BY HAND

Step 1: Mark and cut using the cutting path shown in illustration below. You should have 4 pieces cut out for this style.

1 the bodice front

2 the bodice back

3 4½"-wide piece to be ruffled

4 3"-wide piece to be ruffled

5 2"-wide piece to be ruffled

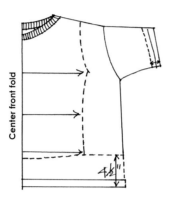

Step 2: Once your pieces are cut out, make sure your rectangle pieces have the same measurements as shown in illustration. Sew a basting stitch 1" from top edge then pull through to achieve your 3 separate ruffles. Remember, do not pull the drawstring too tight.

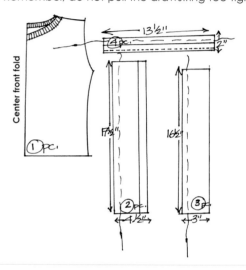

Step 3: Open your pre-cut bodice. Then pin your ruffles to one side. You should stitch each row of ruffles down before proceeding to the next. Sew the largest to the smallest row of ruffles.

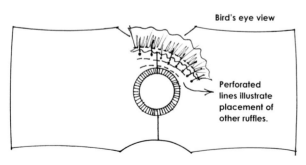

Bird's eye view

Perforated lines illustrate placement of other ruffles.

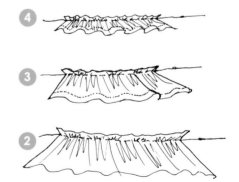

Step 4: Once you have sewn all of your ruffles in place, sew the side seams together. Once again it's your choice whether to do a clean stitch or not. We chose a top stitch for a fun deconstructed look.

It's your option to sew on sequins/paillettes or even cute decorative buttons or gems. Make sure to save this process for last. Do not sew sequin paillettes on before you pull your thread through the drawstring to create ruffles, or the sequins will get lost in the ruffle.

Chapter 18
Quick Quincy

One Shoulder Delight with Lace Detail

You have been roaming town all day in a simple t-shirt and just found out about a party starting about now. With scissors, thread, and simple hand sewing, here's how to remake a t-shirt in 15 minutes or less.

You would think it would take you the entire business day to produce this first-rate garment. Just think, it only took 15 minutes to create this genius and you can even create lace options at a later date. Change the colors of the lace every time you feel necessary. Have a strip of t-shirt in every color of the rainbow. Quickly made, but longevity in your closet. There have been so many times when I (Carmia) left the house to do one thing and ended up doing something else. New York is like that. It pushes you to explore and learn new things. I went grocery shopping, and so wore the plainest of the plainest tee and a cute pair of jeans. I'm grabbing the bare essentials: water, fruit, orange juice, cereal, and poultry when the phone rang. "Carmia, Dave Chapelle is having a secret block party concert in Brooklyn. The Fugees, with L-Boogie, yes, you heard it, L, Kanye West, Common, THE ROOTS, Erykah Badu . . ." My ears were ringing. She had named at least three of my favorite artists. "It starts in a half hour!" How was I going to make it? This was a once in a lifetime concert and I absolutely could not miss it. I dropped the groceries, ran to the ladies room, and created the Quick Quincy tee." I always keep my makeup and basic mini sewing kit in my purse—tricks of the trade, ladies, what can I say. . . Just like your MasterCard, never leave home with it. I beat my face (put on my makeup) and took a taxi to the concert. I arrived looking good and feeling great. My home girl asked me, "When did you have time to shop for a new shirt?" I laughed. I gave her my secret later!

T-shirt Recipe for for Quick Quincy—Shirt on the Go

10 MINUTES WITH MACHINE
15 MINUTES BY HAND

- 1 T-SHIRT ANY SIZE
- HAND SEWING NEEDLES
- IRON
- IRONING BOARD
- SCISSORS
- SEAM RIPPER
- SEWING MACHINE (OPTIONAL)
- SEWING MACHINE NEEDLES (OPTIONAL)
- BOBBINS (OPTIONAL)
- STRAIGHT PINS
- TAILOR'S CHALK
- TAPE MEASURE
- THREAD

DIFFICULTY LEVEL •• 1 •• *So (or sew) easy.*

You can almost make this tee with your eyes closed.

One Shoulder Delight with Lace Detail

10 MINUTES WITH MACHINE • 15 MINUTES BY HAND

Step 1: Mark with tailor's chalk and cut out using cutting path as illustrated below. Save the pieces, to use later as ribbon to be laced through at neckline.

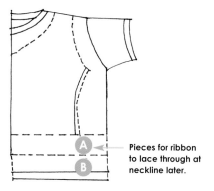

Pieces for ribbon to lace through at neckline later.

Step 2: Open the t-shirt then cut again using the cutting path as shown in illustration.

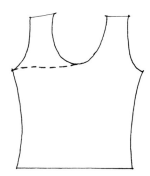

Step 3: Sew your side seams together. You can also jazz things up by using another color on the scraps. The contrast is pretty amazing.

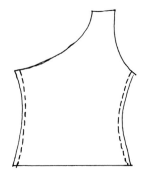

Step 4: Then cut slits along the top of the neck line. Try to space them 1-½" inches apart. However, make sure that the slits at the side shoulder seam are only 1" apart.

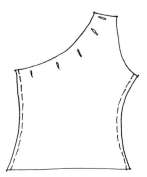

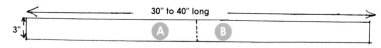

30" to 40" long

3"

A   B

Step 5: Last and final step. Pull long straps through the slits at the top line and you are ready to roll. We suggest tying your bow twice so that it has some volume.

Chapter 19

Missy

Perfect Combination
Kimono Sleeve Tee

The Missy top is outrageously slick. Grand knit bell sleeves attached to a plain t-shirt that is tapered for a slim fit offers an uncommon mix of different textures that works! It is the absolute perfect tee for a chilly day. Its flowing arms are graceful and unexpected. You will need an oversized sweater to create the sleeves. You want the sleeves to look full and glamorous. A sweater too small won't achieve this effect. Any girl can wear this top and pull it off well. The Missy top is universally dapper without a doubt.

In colder temperatures, I (Carmen) am a little less likely to put on a t-shirt alone without an additional layer, such as a sweatshirt, sweater, or cardigan. Although it's cold, I dislike the bulk of more layers for warmth. The Missy Top is praiseworthy. It gives me the comfort of a cotton tee and the warmth of a thermal due to its grandiose bell sleeves. In New York, it gets cold! I refuse to let the winter put a damper on my fashion pride. With my luscious Missy top, I doll up worry-free.

DIFFICULTY LEVEL ●●4●● Challenging.

Trust us, it's worth the trouble.

T-shirt Recipe for Missy—the Perfect Combination Kimono Sleeve Tee

25 MINUTES WITH MACHINE
35 MINUTES BY HAND

- 1 T-SHIRT ANY SIZE
- 1 L OR XL SWEATER
- HAND SEWING NEEDLES
- IRON
- IRONING BOARD
- SCISSORS
- SEAM RIPPER
- SEWING MACHINE (OPTIONAL)
- MACHINE SEWING NEEDLES (OPTIONAL)
- BOBBINS (OPTIONAL)
- STRAIGHT PINS
- TAILOR'S CHALK
- TAPE MEASURE
- THREAD

Perfect Combination Kimono Sleeve Tee

25 MINUTES WITH MACHINE • 35 MINUTES BY HAND

Step 1: Take your t-shirt and cut on the path shown in illustration. Remember: do not cut the crew neck. Pay attention to the raglan sleeve shape. Regard exhibit **A**. It is important to know its measurements for Step 2.

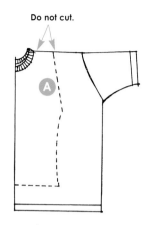

Do not cut.

Step 2: Take your sweater to be used as your palette for the sleeve. Make sure to lay it out completely flat. Absolutely no wrinkles, please! Then follow the cutting path illustrated. Make sure to measure bottom hem width so that you can mark the middle center front of sweater. (THIS IS NOT DIFFICULT, BUT YOU MUST PAY CLOSE ATTENTION AS THERE ARE DETAILS!) See illustration below. Exhibit **B** and **C** should be the same measurements as exhibit **A**. Your center mark for the sleeve has been highlighted. You will have a total of 4 pieces when you finish cutting the shapes from the sweater.

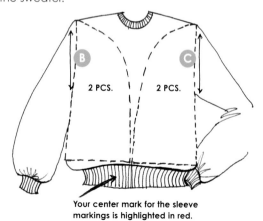

2 PCS.   2 PCS.

Your center mark for the sleeve markings is highlighted in red.

Step 3: This is your front bodice. Remember **A** equals the arm hole where you will attaching the sleeve. (DO NOT PIN OR SEW SIDE SEAMS AT THIS POINT.)

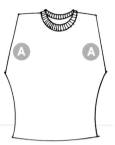

Step 4: Open your bodice top and lay flat. This is in preparation to pin the knit bell sleeves at the arm holes.

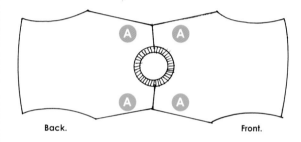

Back.   Front.

Step 5: Open your 4 knit pieces, which will create your sleeves. Place the correct sides together and proceed to sew only the outside seams together. Then measure front arm hole Exhibit **A** in illustration below. Take that Exhibit **A** measurement and mark from the inside top of the sleeves. At the end of that measurement make a notch. Regard illustration below.

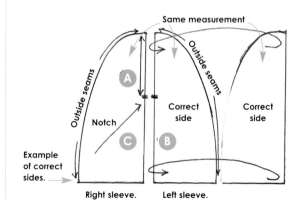

Same measurement

Outside seams

Outside seams

Correct side

Correct side

Notch

Example of correct sides.

Right sleeve.   Left sleeve.

Step 6: After you sew only the outside seams of your sleeves, pin and sew the piece into the arm hole. Remember to flip the sleeves over so correct sides face each other. Make sure that the notches match at the ends before pinning (see exhibit **A** lines on illustration. Note what the sleeve looks like after you flip it over, and pin it before you proceed to sew into arm hole. Remember to use ½" seam allowance.

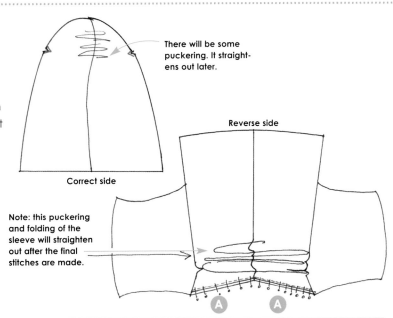

There will be some puckering. It straightens out later.

Reverse side

Correct side

Note: this puckering and folding of the sleeve will straighten out after the final stitches are made.

Step 7: Once both sleeves have been sewn to Exhibit lines **A**, turn the entire shirt inside out. Make sure that all side seams match, then pin. After you pin, then sew together. Regard your sewing path below. Remember you are still giving an ½" seam allowance.

Once all seams are stitched in, secure at all ends. If you have a zigzag stitch on your machine, go back over your knit sleeves with it or if you are sewing by hand go back with a whip stitch.

Reverse side

Inside out reverse side

Reverse side

Whip stitch.

Back.

Zig zag.

Pins out. Turn onto the correct side. And WHAM! You have the perfect top for a cool or cold, crisp winter day.

Chapter 20
Her Highness

Ruffled Neck Halter with Long Sash

This halter has a dramatic ruffled choker made from a man's dress shirt. Its extremely long sash welcomes you to wrap, hang, or twirl as you please! The Her Highness halter top is regal, noble, and poised. It makes you want to stand tall and recognize the style queen in you.

This shirt reminds me (Carmen) of every ballet lesson I've ever had. My shoulders are back, my head is high, and my tee is splendid. It's one of those shirts that commands respect. Nina, a friend of mine, wore the Her Highness top to the 4th of July fireworks at the Piers. It was crowed with thousands of celebrating people. She waited patiently for the sun to set so that the fireworks could begin. Nina admired couples laughing. Families were playing, shouting, and having a great time. However, the shouting became louder and louder—almost unbearable—and she turned around, only to discover they were all looking at her. A group of teenage girls ran up to her. "Excuse Miss, but we just had to tell you that we like your style. Your t-shirt is sweeeeeeeeeet." Nina laughed and thanked the girls profusely. She told them to check out the website, www.sistahsofharlem.com. I was thrilled to hear this story. It's one of the reasons we do this!

DIFFICULTY LEVEL ● ● 4 ● ● *Challenging.*

Collect your badge of honor after you make this one.

T-shirt Recipe for Her Highness— Ruffled Neck Halter with Long Sash

60 MINUTES WITH MACHINE
SEWING MACHINE REQUIRED

- 1 L T-SHIRT
- 1 S OR M WHITE MEN'S DRESS SHIRT (OR ANOTHER COLOR IF YOU DESIRE)
- TAILOR'S CHALK
- THREAD
- IRON
- IRONING BOARD
- HAND SEWING NEEDLES
- STRAIGHT PINS
- SEAM RIPPER
- CLEAR RULER
- TAILOR'S CHALK
- TAPE MEASURE
- ALEENE'S FABRIC GLUE

Ruffled Neck Halter with Long Sash

60 MINUTES WITH MACHINE • SEWING MACHINE REQUIRED

Step 1: For best results use an extra large t-shirt. Mark the shape with tailor's chalk then cut. Regard the cutting path in illustration.

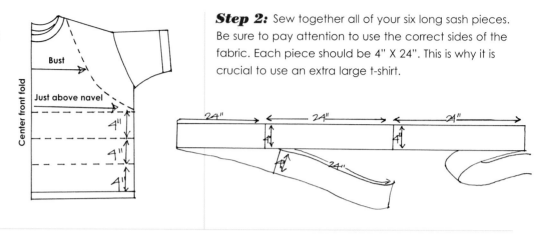

Step 2: Sew together all of your six long sash pieces. Be sure to pay attention to use the correct sides of the fabric. Each piece should be 4" X 24". This is why it is crucial to use an extra large t-shirt.

Step 3: Completely cut the collar from a man's dress shirt (article **A**) Disregard article **B** in illustration at left. Cut the bottom of the dress shirt (article **C**).

Step 4: Sew a basting stitch 1" from the top and cut the edge of article **C**.

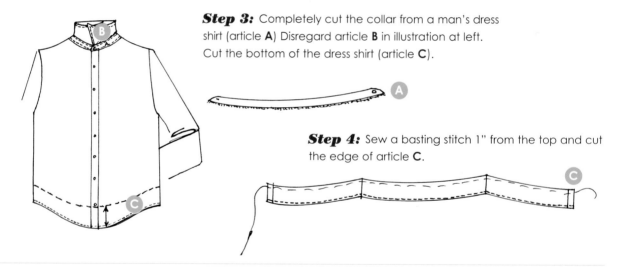

Step 5: After pulling the thread through on article **C**, glue the ruffled collar made from the bottom of the men's dress shirt to Article **A**. Do not glue over the button hole. Let glue dry for approximately 15 minutes. Again, Aleene's fabric glue is recommended.

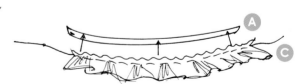

Step 6: While waiting for your collar to dry, sew the extremely long sash. Remember our rule that correct sides must face each other.

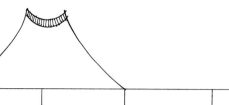

Step 7: Then sew a top stitch over the cotton collar to secure it.

Step 8: Center your collar over the crew neck of the halter. Pin it, then sew it, using a top stitch of a different color thread for that extra pizzaz. And voilà! You have a dramatic halter.

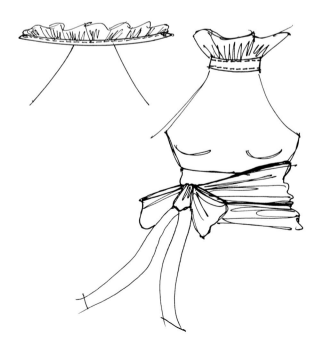

Chapter 21
Rock Star Dress

Rock Star Dress

Who says a t-shirt has to be a shirt? T-shirts make breathtaking dresses that are incredibly comfortable. Style and comfort; who could ask for more?

This is one fantastic t-shirt mini dress! The Rock Star Dress has an asymmetrical neck with mini tie detail. Black mini skirt connected and mesh waistband with side split, like its namesake, is an absolute showstopper! This sweet dress would be described back in the day by New York hip hoppers as bananas! Translation: hot commodity. It's the type of dress that you can easily lay on top of a pair of pants or rock with a pair of leg warmers with a pair of classic Converse Chuck Taylor sneakers. It combines the comfort of a silk nightgown without compromising your savoir-faire. We love when we can look good and not feel trapped in a bottle. The rock star dress promotes full fashion all the way.

DIFFICULTY LEVEL ·· 4 ·· Complex.

A day at the spa with this dress and then appearing ready for dinner without changing clothes, will make up for the effort. There are many steps to creating this style. You are not only using two t-shirts but additional mesh material for a lower hip waist band as well. Taking the accurate measurements is key when creating this style. Unlike other styles in this book, you can NOT "fake" this style. With this baby, the correct cutting is crucial to making it work. The skirt has a draping detail. To attain a fabulous drape, make sure you use an XL and cut precisely on the cutting path. Know your hip measurements to a tee. The drape has to hit at the hip if you want a flowing skirt detail.

T-shirt Recipe for Rock Star Dress

60 MINUTES WITH MACHINE
90 MINUTES BY HAND

- 1 L OR XL T-SHIRT
- 1 L OR XL BLACK T-SHIRT (OR YOU CAN CHOOSE ANOTHER COLOR FOR THE ATTACHED SKIRT)
- ¼" YARD BLACK STRETCH MESH FABRIC
- CLEAR RULER
- SCISSORS
- SEAM RIPPER
- SEWING MACHINE (OPTIONAL)
- SEWING MACHINE NEEDLES (OPTIONAL)
- BOBBINS
- STRAIGHT PINS
- TAILOR'S CHALK
- TAPE MEASURE
- THREAD

Rock Star Dress

Step 1: follow the cutting path in illustration at right for your first t-shirt. Do not cut your side shoulder seams. This should be one long piece. Do not cut center front fold. It will be your collar tie. For your 2'' width cut at side seam. Just cut one side, not both.

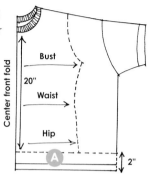

Step 2: After you have cut your front bodice piece, open and unfold, proceed to cut the neck path using the cutting path in illustration. CUT THE FRONT NECKLINE ONLY!

Front bodice.

Step 3: Then cut a small amount of mesh material about 2 inches wide. The width should match the same measurement as your hip. Fold your fabric in half. Mark with a white tailor's chalk and a clear pattern making ruler.

This should measure ½'' of your hip.

Clear pattern making ruler.

Step 4: Now take your second t-shirt in a solid color. We suggest size L or XL for draping. Follow the cutting path. (DO NOT CUT CENTER-FRONT FOLDS.) Remember, it's your choice how long or short you want the dress to fall. These measurements are just examples.

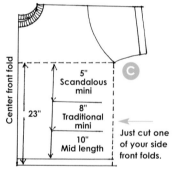

23"

5" Scandalous mini

8" Traditional mini

10" Mid length

Just cut one of your side front folds.

Step 5: Lay your pre-cut front bodice out flat. Then pin and sew the pre-cut collar tie at the neckline. See the illustration. [The sewing is highlighted in blue.] For the collar, only give ¼'' seam allowance. Also remember your correct side of Piece A. It should face the front bodice piece.

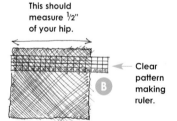

Back.

Front.

Correct side

Correct side

Step 6: After your collar is sewed into place, pin the loose hanging pieces (see article **A**) upward, out of the way. With correct sides facing each other, pin, then sew your side seams together.

Reverse back bodice.

Note: Leave a 1" space at point of the pre-cut neckline. You must do this so that you can tie a knot in that space.

Step 7: Once the side seams are sewn together, turn the top bodice piece back onto the correct side. Then pin and sew mesh strip **B** onto the bottom edge. Follow sewing path in illustration. Remember seam allowance is ½".

NOTE: both sides are usable for mesh materials; they are two-sided.

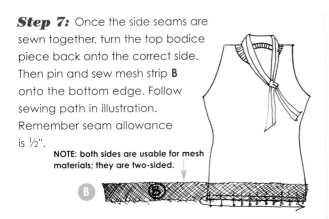

Step 8: After sewing mesh at bottom of the entire top bodice piece, turn the garment inside out. The mesh will need to be sewn together at one side seam. It is such a small distance we don't advise pinning before sewing.

Step 9: Turn your bodice back to the correct side and pin your solid article **C** to the top of the bodice. (REMEMBER, DEPENDING ON THE SIZE OF THE ORINIGAL T-SHIRT, IT WILL EXTEND ANYWHERE FROM 4 TO 6 INCHES, OR MAYBE MORE. BEYOND YOUR HIP MEASUREMENTS.)

Pay close attention to the illustration and sewing path. You will have to make sure that the correct sides of fabric face each other.

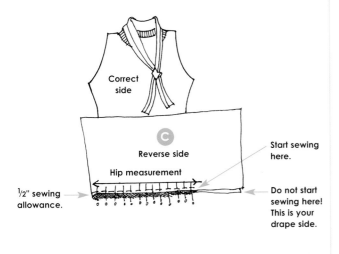

Correct side

Reverse side

C

Hip measurement

½" sewing allowance.

Start sewing here.

Do not start sewing here! This is your drape side.

Step 10: After piece **C** has been sewn on. Flip it back down the correct way. Make a top stitch down the draped side just 3 to 4 inches long.

CLOSE UP DETAIL

Front bodice edge

3" to 4" top stitch.

Front solid piece

C

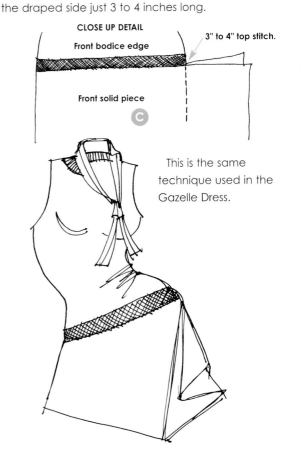

This is the same technique used in the Gazelle Dress.

Chapter 22

Gazelle Dress

Deep V-neck with Ruffled Sleeve Dress

The Gazelle Dress is electrifying! Made from three oversized t-shirts, it has a plunging deep V-neck, open back, and asymmetrical hemline. Dangerous. Cars run red lights when they see this dress. It is vibrant, friendly, and flat out sexy. Pictured in yellow, green, and orange, the slightly ruffled sleeves are ultra feminine; the asymmetrical hemline is daring; and the deep V-neck and open back are bold, dynamic, and fiery. The Gazelle dress is a certified jaw-dropper. Your heart will skip a beat.

Please remember to use three extra-large t-shirts, complementary in color, when creatng the Gazelle dress. Lots of material is required for F&F ("fierce and fab") draping. If the T-shirts used are too small, this dress will not flow. With plenty of oversized tee fabric, you will spin, twirl, and groove in this dress to your own beat.

Magnificent Sistahs enjoy the experience this dress has to offer!

DIFFICULTY LEVEL • • 5 • • *Sewing skils arel a must.*

Time is required, but the payoff is brilliant.

T-shirt Recipe for Gazelle—Deep V-Neck with Ruffled Sleeve Dress

60 MINUTES WITH MACHINE
90 MINUTES BY HAND

- 3 L OR XL T-SHIRTS
- HAND SEWING NEEDLES
- SCISSORS
- SEWING MACHINE REQUIRED
- MACHINE SEWING NEEDLES
- BOBBINS
- STRAIGHT PINS
- TAILOR'S CHALK
- TAPE MEASURE
- THREAD

Deep V-neck with Ruffled Sleeve Dress

60 MINUTES WITH MACHINE • 90 MINUTES BY HAND

Step 1: With your first t-shirt mark and cut as shown in illustration. It is your choice how deep a V-neck you want.

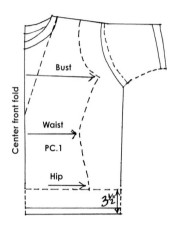

Step 3: Take your second t-shirt and cut as illustrated. We suggest sizes L and XL for a better drape. The angled line should measure half of your hip in inches.

Step 2: Take your two cut sleeve pieces as well as the two 3½"-wide bottom pieces and sew basting stitches 1" from top edge as illustrated. Then pull the thread through to ruffle them.

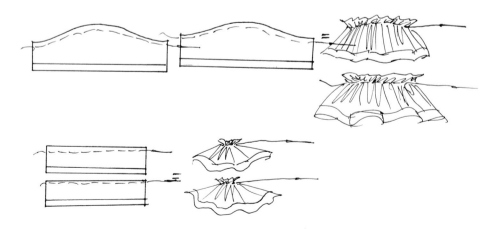

Step 4: Take your third t-shirt and cut as illustrated here which will give you 2 pieces.

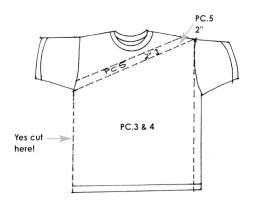

Step 5: Open the top of bodice piece #1 and pin the ruffled cap sleeves onto the arm holes, then top stitch down. Remember to sew the larger ruffles on first. Then cut 2 small slits for strap from piece #5. Then pull piece #5 through slits and knot.

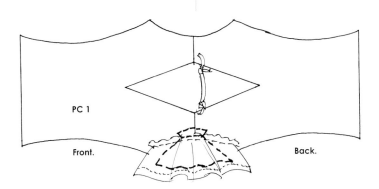

Deep V-neck with Ruffled Sleeve Dress

60 MINUTES WITH MACHINE • 90 MINUTES BY HAND

Step 6: After the ruffled cap sleeves have been top-stitched into place, fold the bodice with correct sides facing each other. Then pin and sew the side seams together. Remember to use ½" seam allowance.

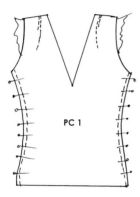

PC 1

Step 7: Sew the pre-cut bottom pieces (**2**, **3**, and **4**) to each other as illustrated below. Piece **#2** is illustrated open and unfolded for better understanding. Remember to place pieces face to face so that you have clean seams, not deconstructed top stitched ones.

Step 8: Turn your top bodice back to the correct side. Then fold and turn the bottom skirt piece upward and pin to bottom of bodice as illustrated.

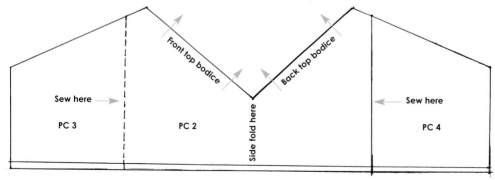

Sew here →

PC 3

Front top bodice

Side fold here

Back top bodice

PC 2

← Sew here

PC 4

Step 9: Lay the dress flat, then sew a top stitch straight from side seams where it opens for draping. The top stitch should be 6½" or longer.

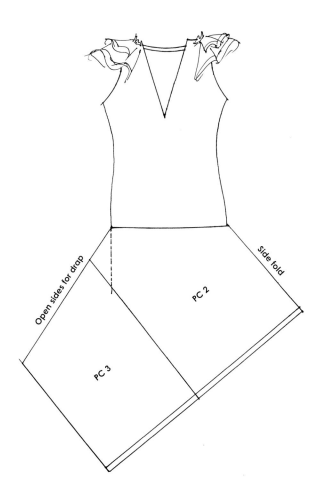

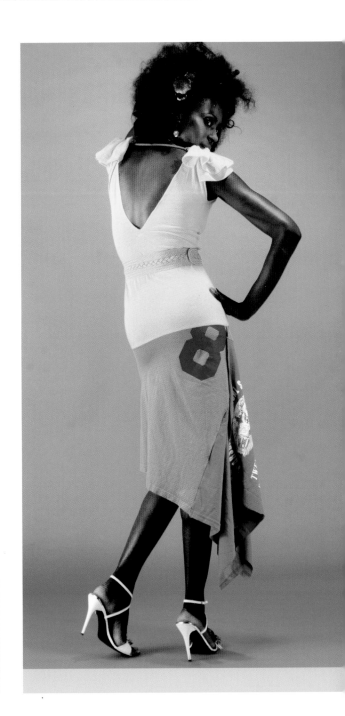

Chapter 23

Simply White

V-neck Top with Draping Detail

Let's do a solid. It's classic. A simple white tee can save an outfit. But it doesn't have to be simple. Now it's time to jazz it up. Let your white t-shirt keep the crowd guessing. "Where did she get that shirt?"

The simply white shirt has been reworked into a raw edge V-neck with delightful shoulder ties. Turn around; the back is striking. Individual t-shirt laces drape remarkably down the back of this tee. It's flawless eye candy for those who crave something sweet.

We like to call this the "surprise" shirt. From the front, you see a basic V-neck white tee with delicate shoulder straps. It's clean, straightforward, and pretty. You turn around and BAM, gorgeous laces envelope your entire back. It brings forth the excitement that we crave when dressing to the nines.

The great thing about this shirt: you can change the laces. Try different colored t-shirt laces that can be made quickly and easily from other old tees. Also consider replacing your t-shirt laces with ritzy cords. A cord is a string or small rope of several strands twisted together. (You can purchase cords from your local trimming store. They come in various sizes.) In fact, your laces can be any lightweight fabric material. Explore all of your options, such as lace, ribbon, suede, and silk. Try adding a myriad of lace types to your Simply White Tee; you can make this style even more off the hook. We say, "never hold back!"

T-shirt Recipe for Simply White— V-Neck Top with Draping Detail

15 MINUTES WITH MACHINE
25 MINUTES BY HAND

- 1 M OR L WHITE T-SHIRT
- HAND SEWING NEEDLES
- IRON
- IRONING BOARD
- SCISSORS
- SEAM RIPPER
- SEWING MACHINE (OPTIONAL)
- SEWING MACHINE NEEDLES (OPTIONAL)
- BOBBINS (OPTIONAL)
- STRAIGHT PINS
- TAILOR'S CHALK
- THIMBLE
- THREAD

DIFFICULTY LEVEL • • 3 • • *Sewing 101 is useful.*

Creating this diva is more imagination and verve than sewing skill.

V-neck Top with Draping Detail

15 MINUTES WITH MACHINE • 25 MINUTES BY HAND

Step 1: Use a large or XL t-shirt for this style. Mark and cut out as demonstrated in illustration. Remember that your V-neck can be daring and low, or higher and not so revealing.

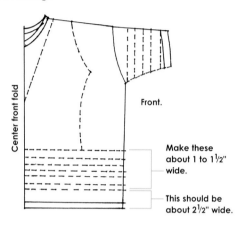

Center front fold

Front.

Make these about 1 to 1½" wide.

This should be about 2½" wide.

Step 2: Once your bodice top is cut out, cut tiny slits along he V-neck line. Be careful not to cut too close to the edge. And do not make slits larger than ½". You will have twelve long 1" straps, ten short straps, and two long 2½" straps.

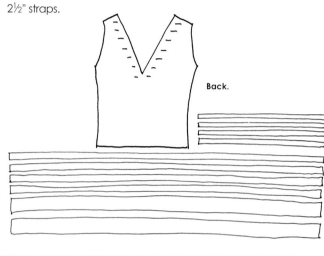

Back.

Step 3: Then take all of your scraps and pull them on both ends so that they curl on each edge, giving them a more cord-like appeal.

Step 4: Turn your precut shirt around to the front then pin your sides so that you can secure the top before sewing. For more fun, use a multicolored thread. Also, we suggest a top stitch for this style. If your sewing machine has a zig zag stitch, use it! But remember when pinning for a zig zag stitch, your straight pins should be vertical not horizontal. Regard exhibit **A** in illustration.

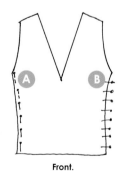

Front.

Step 5: Once you have sewn your side seams together, pull your laces through the slits at the back V-neck shape. Use random numbers of laces in each set of slits. For example, we placed 2-3 laces in some sets of slits and just tied knots at the end so that they are secure. Use the smaller, shorter laces as you get closer to the bottom of the deep V-neck shape. For the last 2 slits, we tied the shortest laces vertically.

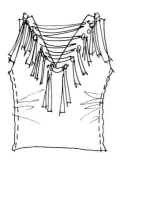 

Side view.

Step 6: Now for your last step. Take those 2 wider 2½" laces and tie them at the front shoulder seams. Regard the illustration. Let one part of the strap hang to the front and the other hang to the back.

Chapter 24
*Un*basic Black

Unbasic Black

Here's how to make black t-shirts fun. Even in a cluster of dark colors, this black t-shirt will receive a standing ovation. The unbasic black tee is a boat neck blouson style with charming sliced shoulder details. It's Coco Chanel meets Sistahs of Harlem. This black tee is exquisite and graceful. Let it hang off the shoulder if you're feeling sultry. It gives your everyday jeans quintessential form. The unbasic black tee is perfect for high tea in some of London's most swank tea houses. It's brilliant for Sunday brunch with the girls. This creation is also flattering on all body types. Its blouson style and slightly fitted waist are a total thumbs up.This shirt is a class act. Our survey says, "Poised to Perfection."

DIFFICULTY LEVEL •• 4 •• Challenging.

It's worth it. You can wear this shirt for the rest of your life.

T-shirt Recipe for Unbasic Black

30 MINUTES WITH MACHINE
45 MINUTES BY HAND

- 1 XL BLACK T-SHIRT
- HAND SEWING NEEDLES
- IRON
- IRONING BOARD
- SCISSORS
- SEAM RIPPER
- SEWING MACHINE (OPTIONAL)
- SEWING MACHINE (NEEDLES)
- STRAIGHT PINS
- TAILOR'S CHALK
- TAPE MEASURE

Unbasic Black

30 MINUTES WITH MACHINE • 45 MINUTES BY HAND

Step 1: Mark and cut your top using the cutting path in illustration. Make sure that your side top shoulder seam is between 1½" - 2" wide. It is very important to pay careful attention to the measurements.

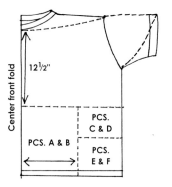

Step 3: Unfold pieces **A** and **B**, which will become your high empire waistband. Place them correct side to correct side (i.e.: inside-out) because we want clean seams from this style. These pieces, once you unfold and open, will be half your waist measurement.

For example, if your waist is 27, then it would be 13 ÷ ½ + 1. Remember: how you pin depends on whether your are sewing by hand or by machine.

Once you have finished pinning, proceed to sew the side seams together using a ½" seam allowance.

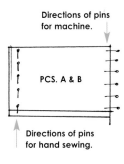

Directions of pins for machine.

PCS. A & B

Directions of pins for hand sewing.

Step 2: Now that you have cut your pieces out, unfold and open the top bodice piece. Then sew a basting stitch 1" from the bottom edge as shown in illustration. Then pull the thread through to gather. Do not gather it too tight; you must be able to get into the top. Measure the opening and make it 1" to 2" more than your bust.

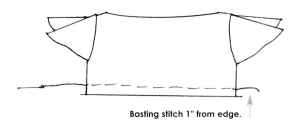

Basting stitch 1" from edge.

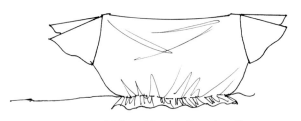

Pull thread through, like a drawstring.

Step 4: Pin and sew your empire waist—which is made up of pieces **A** and **B**—to your top boat neck bodice. See illustration.

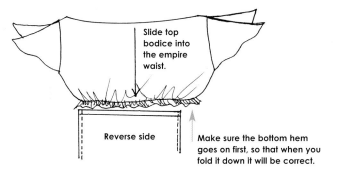

Slide top bodice into the empire waist.

Reverse side

Make sure the bottom hem goes on first, so that when you fold it down it will be correct.

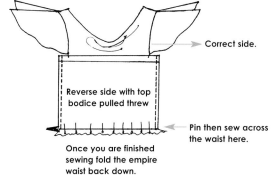

Correct side.

Reverse side with top bodice pulled threw

Pin then sew across the waist here.

Once you are finished sewing fold the empire waist back down.

Step 5: Take pieces **C** through **F** and sew 1" into them over the side just above the center of he slits of the pair sleeves. This is that extra fabric for flashy, draping appeal. Regard illustration. Slide the top bodice into the empire waist. Make sure the bottom hem goes on first, so when you fold it down, it is correct.

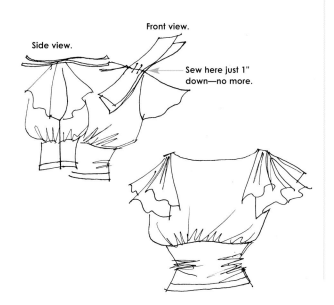

Side view.

Front view.

Sew here just 1" down—no more.

Resources

T-shirts (L and XL are highly recommended.)

Local Salvation Army or Goodwill
Family's and friends' closets
Your closet
Flea markets
Church 2nd hand sales
Swap parties with friends
Yard Sales
Local vintage boutiques
www.americanapparel.com
www.target.com
www.kmart.com
www.modells.com
www.sears.com
www.walmart.com
www.t-shirt.com
www.defunker.com

Trimming

www.mjtrim.com
www.FashionFabricsOnline.com
www.DistinctiveFabric.com
www.GalaxyTrim.com
www.fabric.com
www.butts4u.com ($15 minimum)
www.cybertrim.com

Findings and Basic Sewing Supplies

www.JoAnn.com
www.SewTrue.com
www.michaels.com
www.pearlpaint.com

The One-Stop Wardrobe Supply Shop

www.WardrobeSupplies.com

Where to Find Sistahs of Harlem Apparel

Sistahs of Harlem online boutque:
www.sistahsofharlem.com

Addy & Ferreo
672 Fulton Street
Brooklyn, NY 11217
718-248-2900

Pieces of Harlem
228 W. 135 Street
New York, NY 10030
212-234-1725

Superdeluxe
187 Chrystie Street
New York, NY 10002
212-529-0101

Lil Limo
4-5-4 2F Nishi-azabu
Minato-ku, Tokyo 106-0031
Japan 03.5464.2568

Article & Irie
Japan

Visual Glossary

Necklines

Jewel

Scoop

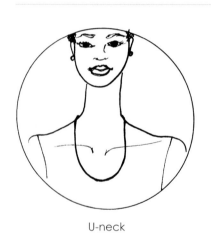

U-neck

V-neck

Square-neck

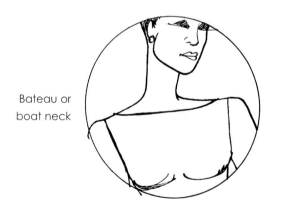

Bateau or boat neck

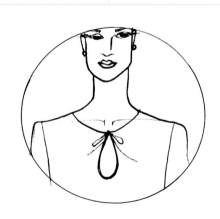

Keyhole

Drape

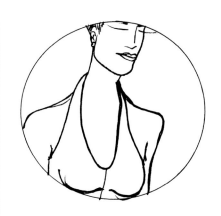

Halter

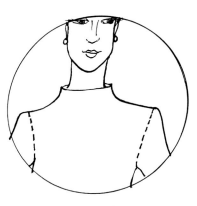

Funnel

Crew-neck

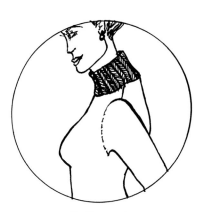

Turtle-neck

Cowl-neck

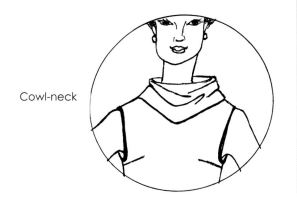

Traditional
tank top

Visual Glossary

Sleeves

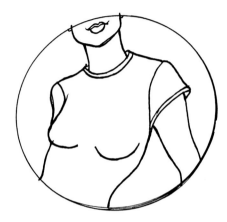

Cap sleeve

Puff sleeve

Ruffled cap sleeve

Bishop sleeve

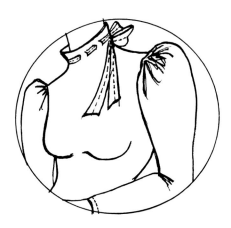

Leg of mutton sleeve

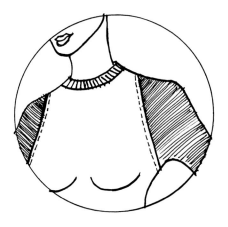

Raglan sleeve

Kimono sleeve

Bell sleeve

Glossary

accent: emphasis or prominence given to a line or decorative color in costume

accessory: an object, i.e., purse, earrings, legwarmers, scarf, etc, that can be added to give an ensemble character

A-line: slightly flared from the narrow waist or shoulders

basic sewing equipment: the essential item required for constructing apparel; assorted fasteners, sewing machine needles, buttons, seam ripper, safety pins, hand sewing needles, needle threader, tailor's chalk, thimble, tape measure, thread, pin holder

basting stitch: large, easy stitches used to hold fabric in place temporarily

bodice: The fitted part of a shirt or dress that extends from the waist to the shoulder

bobbin: thread carrier used in sewing machines

care label: the care label is a required label in which manufacturers and importers provide at least one satisfactory method of care necessary for the ordinary use of the garment. Most labels include fabric, content, cleaning and ironing instructions, and the region where the garment was made.

carotene (yellow): An orange-yellow to red crystalline pigment; yellow undertones for your skin; one of three pigments used to determine your skin tone

center back fold: (on the back part of shirt) match up the sleeve insets (armpits), and fold your t-shirt directly in half. Replace it on the ironing board. This creates the center back fold, also known as C.B.F. The center back fold is one of the formulas from which pattern drafting originates.

center front fold: (on the front part of shirt) Match up the sleeve insets (armpits), and fold your t-shirt directly in half. Replace it on the ironing board. This creates the center front fold also know as C.F.F. The center front fold is one of the formulas from which pattern drafting originates.

clean seam: seam stitched and pressed open; looks invisible, from a distance; when view closely looks like a straight line

complementary colors: colors on the opposite side of the color wheel, i.e. red/green, blue/orange, yellow/purple

cord: string or small rope of several strands twisted together

cummerbund: broad-fitted sash which fits around the waist usually worn with a tuxedo

cut: style or manner in which garment is separated

cord: a string or small rope of several strands twisted together

couture: French word meaning sewing or needlework; the business of designing, making, and selling highly fashionable, usually custom-made clothing for women; the high-fashion clothing created by designers.

cutting path: the line that you follow and cut when creating the shape of your garments, accessories, etc.

deconstruction: taking apart an existing garment, or accessory, and transforming it into something else, i.e., old tie becomes belt; a t-shirt becomes a halter; a t-shirt becomes skirt, etc..; raw edges

drawstring: a string in the seam of the material which can be pulled to tighten

embellishments: adornments, decorative items, i.e., sequins, jewels, trimming, etc.

empire waist: garments with an extremely high waist, usually 2 to 4 inches above the navel on pants, skirts, shorts, etc.

embroidery shears: scissors used to cut embellished fabric, material, or garments

epaulet: shoulder ornament or trimming designed to give width to shoulder

fabric glue: adhesive used especially for fabric

fastener: device that fastens or holds together separate fabric parts

findings: threads, tapes, buttons, binding, hook and eyes, slide fasteners, featherbone, belting, braids, and other sewing essentials used in garment making

hem: finish provided by turning the raw edges under from $\frac{1}{8}$ to $\frac{1}{2}$ inch; secured by hand or sewing machine

hemming tape: adhensive strip $\frac{1}{2}$ inch-wide, used for hemming; applied at the fold of the garment for a quick hem

hemoglobin: a hemoprotein composed of globin and heme that gives red blood cells their characteristic color (red); function primarily to transport oxygen from the lungs to the body tissues; one of the three elements that determine your skin tone

hook & eyes: type of fastener in two pieces, a hook and a loop which link together to secure the closing on garments

interfacing: a moderately stiff/firm material used between layers of fabric to thicken or stiffen it

kimono: garment typical of Japanese culture;, made as loose wide-sleeved robe fastened around waist with broad sash

kimono sleeve: grandiose bell sleeve similar to sleeves on a *furisode*, long-sleeve kimono

mark: A visible trace or impression, such as a line using tailor's chalk, illustrating where the fabric is to be cut; indicates measurements

measure: the act of measuring; to mark, lay out, or establish dimensions by measuring

melanin (brown): any group of naturally occurring dark pigments in the hair, skin, fur, feathers, or iris of the eye; it is responsible for the tanning of skin exposed to light

Glossary

monochromatic: containing or using one color

notch(es): an indentation or incision on an edge, used to indicate where to cut fabric

paillettes: pieces of glittery, ritzy materials used to embellish and adorn your tees

pleat: a double or multiple fold in a garment or other garments made from cloth; fabric normally laid back, flat, and held together by stitching at the top or the side

primary colors: red, yellow, blue

pin holder: cushion or cloth pad used to carry various pins, mostly likely straight pins

obi: broad Japanese sash

raw edge: unfinished seam or edge of fabric

ribbing: arrangement of ribs; raised rows of fabric arranged vertically or horizontally

ruffle: A strip of frilled or closely gathered fabric used for trimming or decoration

ruche: a ruffle or pleat of lace, muslin, or other fine fabric used for trimming women's garments

salvage: to save or recover from destruction

sash: ornamental band, scarf, strip, or belt worn around the waist or over the shoulders

seam: joining line where parts of a garment are sewed together

seam allowance: The seam allowance is the distance between the seam line (stitching line) that joins two or more pieces of fabric together and the cut edge of the fabric.

seam ripper: a small device with a small hook used to remove stitches from a garment or fabric; opens almost any seam effortlessly

seam tape: seam ribbon about $\frac{1}{2}$ inch-wide used for finishing the top of hems, sleeve edges, etc.

seasons of color: winter, spring, summer, autumn

secondary colors: orange, green, purple

secure stitch: when coming to the end of a stitch, sew back over it $\frac{1}{8}$ inch; if using a sewing machine, press the reverse handle while stiching; if sewing by hand, sew backwards, repeat, and place another stitch on top of the already existing stitch

sewing machine: A machine for sewing, often having additional attachments for special stitching

sewing weights: small weights used to anchor fabric while cutting or sewing material

shears: a pair of scissors used to cut or remove fabirc

silhouette: shape or outline of natural body

short waisted: Having a distance between shoulders and waist that is shorter than average; short torso

stitch: single turn or loop of the yarn or thread by hand or by machine in sewing

stiching line: the actual line that you are sewing

snap tape: firmly woven tape to which snap fasteners are securely anchored

safety pin: A pin in the form of a clasp, having a sheath to cover and hold the point; used for joining separate pieces

straight pin: pin consisting of a short, straight stiff piece of wire with a pointed end; used to fasten pieces of cloth or paper together

style: particular cut, design, or type of an article

tailor's chalk: A piece of clay or wax in crayon form, used for marking on a fabric to indicate

the cutting line, measurements, etc. Clay brushes out of fabric, and wax will melt off with the iron

tape measure: a length of tape or thin flexible metal, marked at intervals for measuring

thimble: cap or covering used to protect end of finger in sewing; usually worn on second finger

thread: slender cord of varying degrees of fineness, produced by twisting together two or more filaments spun from cotton, flax, silk, nylon, or other fibers

tracing paper: semi-transparent paper used for tracing, drawing, designs, maps, etc.

tracing wheel: an unusually toothed wheel with a handle that is used on tracing paper to trace a sewing pattern on tracing paper

trimming: decoration or ornamental parts; also, act of applying such decorations

undertones: subtle pale or subdued color underneath your skin;

undertones are determined by the combination of three pigments: melanin (brown), carotene (yellow), hemoglobin (red)

velcro: fabric hook-and-loop fasteners used for connecting objects; used for a closure consisting of a piece of fabric of small hooks that sticks to a corresponding fabric of small loops

waist: line around the part of the human figure between the shoulder and hip that is most contracted

whip stitch: short, easy, overcasting used to sew 2 seams together; not an invisible stitch; often decorative

zig zag stitch: chain stitch made by inserting needle at an angle and altering from side to side; looks similar to inverted letter Z

zipper: A fastening device consisting of parallel rows of metal, plastic, or nylon teeth on adjacent edges of an opening that are interlocked by a sliding tab

Credits

Chapter 5: Elizabeth
Photographer:
www.derrickgomez.com
Hair: Deigo Silva
Makeup: Shade Boyewa
Earrings: by Metal Monk
Bracelets: by Kimiwear
Model: Meagan @ Ikon

Chapter 6: Theresa
Photographer:
www.derrickgomez.com
Hair: Deigo Silva
Makeup: Shade Boyewa
Earrings: by Alexis Bittar
Bracelets: by Kimiwear
Model: Deonna @ Ohm

Chapter 7: Francesca
Photographer:
www.derrickgomez.com
Hair: Deigo Silva
Makeup: Shade Boyewa
All accessories: by Alexis Bittar
Model: Sun @ Ohm

Chapter 8: Cuban Disco
Photographer: Oliverie
Hair: by Dana Gibbs
Makeup: Shade Boyewa
Accessories: by Kimiwear
Model: Kindra (freelance)

Chapter 9: Cairo
Photograher: Olivere
Hair: by Dana Gibbs
Makeup: Shade Boyewa
Accessories: by Kimiwear
Model: Cheyanne @ Q Models

Chapter 10: Bella
Photographer: Olivere
Hair: by Dana Gibbs
Makeup: Shade Boyewa
Accessories: by Kimiwear
Model: Kindra (Freelance)

Chapter 11: Miami
Photographer: Oliverie
Hair: by Dana Gibbs
Makeup: Shade Boyewa
Accessories: by Kimiwear
Model: Cheyanne @ Q Models

Chapter 12: Kyoko
Photographer:
www.derrickgomez.com
Hair: Deigo Silva
Makeup: Shade Boyewa
Earrings: by Metal Monk
Bracelets: by Kimiwear
Model: Sun @ Ohm

Chapter 13: Margarita
Photographer: Olivereie
Hair: by Dana Gibbs
Makeup: Shade Boyewa
Accessories: by Kimiwear
Model: Cheyanne @ Q Models

Chapter 14: Daddy Bruce
Photographer:
www.derrickgomez.com
Hair: Deigo Silva
Makeup: Shade Boyewa
Earrings: by Kimina Baylli
Bracelets: by Alexis Bittar
Model: Keisha (Freelance)

Chapter 15: Pocahantas
Photographer:
www.derrickgomez.com
Hair: Deigo Silva
Makeup: Shade Boyewa
Earrings: by Kimina Bayilli
Bracelets: by Kimiwear
Model: Sun @ Ohm
Earrings: by Kimina Baylli
Bracelets: by Alexis Bittar
Model: Sun @ Ohm

Chapter 16: Vintage Remix
Photographer:
www.derrickgomez.com
Hair: Deigo Silva
Makeup: Shade Boyewa
Bracelet left arm: by Alexis Bittar
Bracelet right arm: by Kimiwear
Model: Deonna @ Ohm

Chapter 17: Haile
Photographer:
www.derrickgomez.com
Hair: Deigo Silva
Makeup: Shade Boyewa
Earrings: by Kimiwear
Model: Meagan @ Ikon

Chapter 18: Quick Quincy
Photographer:
www.derrickgomez.com
Hair: Deigo Silva
Makeup: Shade Boyewa
Earrings: by Alexis Bittar
Bracelets: by Kimiwear
Model: Deonna @ Ohm

Chapter 19: Missy
Photographer: Ernesto Urdanete
Hair: DJ Riggs
Makeup: Ayinde Castro
Model: Lak (Freelance)
Art Direction: Rina Malonzo @
Tink Tank

Chapter 20: Her Highness
Photographer:
www.derrickgomez.com
Hair: Deigo Silva
Makeup: Shade Boyewa
All accessories: by Alexis Bittar
Model: Meagan @ Ikon
Management

Chapter 21: Rock Star Dress
Photographer: Ernesto Urdanete
Hair: Dana Gibbs
Makeup: Ayinde Castro
Bracelets: by Kimiwear
Model: Lak (Freelance)
Art Direction: Rina Malonzo @
Tink Tank

Chapter 22: Gazelle Dress
Photographer:
www.derrickgomez.com
Hair: Deigo Silva
Makeup: Shade Boyewa
All accessories: by Alexis Bittar
Model: Keisha (Freelance)

Chapter 23: Simply White
Photographer:
www.derrickgomez.com
Hair: Deigo Silva
Makeup: Shade Boyewa
All accessories: by Alexis Bittar
Model: Keisha (Freelance)

Chapter 24: Unbasic Black
Photographer:
www.derrickgomez.com
Hair: Deigo Silva
Makeup: Shade Boyewa
Accessories: Sterling silver cubes
w/ large black fabric-covered
beads. Hairpiece & earrings by
Alexis Bittar; gold and onyx neck-
lace, white and black necklace
by Kimina Baylli
Model: Sun @ Ohm Models

Acknowledgments

THANK YOU TO OUR BROTHERS, SISTERS, AND DAD

OUR MOTHERS:

Betty Jean, my mother and my best friend, I love you so much, Thanks for your unconditional support and wisdom. You're the sweetest and most reliable person in the world.

Libbie Webber, confidante/spiritual guidance/mentor, I love you me-maw.

OUR BROTHERS AND SISTERS:

Takiyah, you're the best sister in the world. Can't imagine life without you.

Cherod Webber, Maurice Webber, and Winston Webber for lending an ear during the more challenging times.

OUR FRIENDS AND FAMILY:

Carmencita, thanks for being our #1 cheerleader. Love you much.

The Bradley sisters, forever friends. Thanks for helping me to stand strong.

Samiayah. You are the honorary 3rd Sistah of Harlem. If we can count on anyone, we can count on you! We love you, girl!

Jackie. Your way with words is profound. Page 9 belongs to you.

Diane Gedymin. You planted this idea in our head and look what grew from it. Thank you.

Adrienne Ingrum. Thanks for believing and pushing us in the right direction—FORWARD. You ALWAYS believed in us!! You always knew that this book would happen. We have learned so much from you and look forward to a lifelong partnership.

Marta Hallett, Glitterati Incorporated rocks! Thanks for giving us a venue to share our ideas. You are a true visionary. We have to do this again and again!

In the beginning, Iman you opened so many doors for us. For that, we are forever grateful. Thanks!

The vanity team: Shade Boyewa, Dana Gibbs, Diego Silva, Ayinde Castro, thanks for helping us create the pretty pictures.

Thanks Derrick Gomez for all of the sleepless nights. Your photography is magnificent.

Rina Malonzo, thanks for your magnificent vision. You put together a great team.

David Yoon, your art direction is genius and you work faster than lightning.

Nancy, thanks for working hard and never complaining.

Audrey Dussard, we truly appreciate you.

Fabulous models: Deonna, Keisha, Lak, Kindra, Cheyenne, Sun, and Meagan. Y'all rock the revamped t-shirts. You look fierce and fab!

Vincent Falls for being a great mentor.

Michaela Angela Davis for all of your words of wisdom.

Ionia Dunn Lee for always remembering us.

N'dea Davenport, you work the clothes, and we love you for it. Thanks for the unconditional support.

Alexis Bittar, thanks for your words of wisdom and encouragement. Your jewelry is absolutely stunning. It brightens any room.

Kimina Baylli - we love your accessories. Thanks for sharing.

Kimberley of Kimi Wear – We love your accessories. We can't get enough. Thanks for being one of our biggest promoters. Love you much.

Dr. Spurgen Webber III for your support.

Nelson Richards of Intellectual Alchemy, you're great. Thanks for your support.

Erica & Vanese from Addy & Ferro, your boutique has the coolest threads. I'm glad that we can be a part.

Latisha and Colin, Pieces of Harlem boutique puts emerging designers on the map. Thanks for loving our threads!

Marilyn of Lil Limo in Japan. You helped to make us an international brand.

Nichelle Sanders, you're brilliant. Thanks for sticking with Sistahs.

We saw it in a dream. It was a simple idea. It's no longer a dream but a tangible reality. What an amazing feeling! To think it and do it! Dreams do come true with diligence, resilience, and perseverance!!! It takes a village to make a crafts book.

Thank you God for giving us strength and vision.

To those who we forgot to thank, please blame the head not the heart!

Carmen & Carmia